AND NOW FOR SOMETHING
COMPLETELY DIGITAL

THE COMPLETE
ILLUSTRATED GUIDE TO
MONTY PYTHON
CDs AND DVDs

Published by The Disinformation Company Ltd.
163 Third Avenue, Suite 108,New York, NY 10003
Tel.: +1.212.691.1605 Fax: +1.212.691.1606
www.disinfo.com

Library of Congress Control Number: 2006921763
ISBN-13: 978-1-932857-31-3 ISBN-10: 1-932857-31-1
Text Design & Layout: Browns/NYC
Printed in UK 10 9 8 7 6 5 4 3 2 1

Editor: Jason Louv
Cover Ilustrations: Brian Paisley
Back Cover Design: Jacob Rosette
Production Editor: Maya Shmuter
Managing Editor: Ralph Bernardo

Distributed in the USA and Canada by:
Consortium Book Sales and Distribution
1045 Westgate Drive, Suite 90 St Paul, MN 55114
Toll Free: +1.800.283.3572 Local: +1.651.221.9035
Fax: +1.651.221.0124 www.cbsd.com

Distributed in the United Kingdom and Eire by: Virgin Books
Thames Wharf Studios, Rainville Road London W6 9HA
Tel.: +44.(0)20.7386.3300 Fax: +44.(0)20.7386.3360
E-Mail: sales@virgin-books.co.uk

Distributed in Australia by: Tower Books
Unit 2/17 Rodborough Road,
Frenchs Forest, NSW 2086
Tel.: +61.2.9975.5566 Fax: +61.2.9975.5599
Email: towerbks@zip.com.au

AND NOW FOR SOMETHING COMPLETELY DIGITAL

THE COMPLETE ILLUSTRATED GUIDE TO MONTY PYTHON CDs AND DVDs

WRITTEN BY
ALAN PARKER & MICK O'SHEA

ACKNOWLEDGEMENTS

In the first place we'd like to thank Michael Palin, Terry Jones, Terry Gilliam, John Cleese, Eric Idle, Neil Innes, Carol Cleveland, Andre Jacquemin and the late Graham Chapman (for inspiration alone).

Olive Parker (Alan's mum) — thanks for everything.

David Parker (Alan's brother) — and so it comes to pass that when two or three are gathered together they will perform the 'Parrot' sketch! Robert Kirby at Peters, Fraser and Dunlop (Alan's agent and our guide). Steve Woof at EMI Records; Daz, Andy, Chris and Drew at the Red Room; Sean Body and Graham at Helter Skelter Books; Gary, Dave, Liz, Jacob, Jason, Maya, Ralph and Richard at Disinformation (without whom); Graham at Browns/NYC; Stina and Alex at Virgin Books; Jake Burns, Steve Grantley, Ian McCallum and Bruce Foxton (Stiff Little Fingers); Shirley Sexton at slf.com; Zoe Street; Jerry White; Terry Rawlings; Welsh Pete; Gary Crowley; Jim McDonald; Steve 'Roadent' Connolly; Rob Harvey; Chris Remington; Don Letts; Kate Furey; Martin Baker; Rock n' Roll Ray Morrissey; Foxy Roxy Gregory; David Morgan and his incredible volume Monty Python Speaks!; *Roger Saunders at Python (Monty) Pictures; Victoria Milton-Knight; Helen Totton; Matt Martin on the stool near the bar; Paul Roberts; Brian Jackson; Catherine Cameron and everybody at Peters, Fraser and Dunlop; Jon Richards; Amy Gilliam; Nomtia; Jon McCaughey; Robert Ross, whose knowledge on this subject helped our research incredibly (you're the boss, mate); Frank Lea at Secret Music; Rav Singh; Bob McCabe (and possibly the best Python book in the history of the world); Paul Dawson and his team at the Cinema Store (London); Tom Kirk and Lee Price at Vivienne Westwood; Gary Carverhill at Grip Design; Laura and Emily at Scruffy Bird PR; Kirk Brandon; Phil Hendriks; Debs and Sarah at EMI Press; everyone at the Spice of Life boozer. Some photographs in this volume are from Private Memorabilia Collections (photographed by Joe Alverez).*

For reasons that will become apparent in the text, this book is dedicated with thanks to Steve Diggle.

CONTENTS

INTRODUCTION: THE LIFE OF A PYTHON NUT

Becoming a Monty Python fan, all those years ago now, was dead easy. Halfway through my first viewing of the 'Parrot' sketch, they had me hook, line and sinker. Monty Python was the first rock n' roll comedy team, in my opinion. I'd heard *The Goon Show* on radio repeats and been impressed with what I'd listened to, but I had no desire to own all their albums. In later years, *Not the Nine O'clock News* had me in tears of laughter, but I never felt the urge to wear the T-shirt. With the Pythons it was different. There's a true story concerning a holiday to New York in June 2002 which ended with me having to buy another suitcase, just to bring home my newly purchased *Monty Python and the Holy Grail* action figures!

"Really?" asked Terry Jones, when I brought him up to speed on the facts at Redwood Studios in London, on a cold winter's day in February 2005. "Yeah," I replied. "Really, I guess that's why the girls who travelled with me thought I was mad!"

Then, of course, there was the release of the movie *Life of Brian*, which was banned by the Bishop of Blackburn, my hometown. At the time, a bunch of us travelled to Blackpool for a screening at the town's long defunct Odeon cinema – what a day that was. "There's still time to save your souls!" shouted one member of the town's women's guilds, dressed not unlike a Python 'pepper pot' lady, as we climbed the steps to the cinema. In a scene mad enough to be straight out of a Python

One of my most prized possesions, thanks Terry!

television sketch, they waved banners at us and shouted things about finding a place in heaven and peace with God! On another trip to New York, in 2003, I caught a screening during a film festival, with my path to the cinema obstructed by nobody. It's amazing the difference a few years can make...

This, then, is the story of six men – five English and one American – who, in the space of forty-five half-hour television shows, transmitted on BBC at a variety of times (pretty near commercial suicide at the beginning) from the late Sixties till the early Seventies; four full-length feature films; a bunch of albums; the odd single; and some pretty impressive books, transformed everything we know about comedy today. They were translated into German twice (*Monty Python's Fliegender Zirkus*), banned on the big screen and played 'sold out' shows at the Hollywood Bowl, just like the Beatles.

I was in Redwood studios on 24 June 2005 when I got the news that my father had passed away. My good friend Steve Diggle of the Buzzcocks rang me – "Stay in town," he said, "I'm on my way." In the weeks that followed I'd put out a kind of SOS among my friends. I wanted to keep busy 24/7 to keep my mind off everything else. During these few weeks an awful lot of deals were struck, and many plans laid. It was Python producer Andre Jacquemin who suggested doing a book on the world's greatest comedy team, and my good mate Mick O'Shea who helped turn the idea into a reality. In what seemed like two minutes after we'd had the idea, we also had a publishing deal (blame the success of *Spamalot* on Broadway). I was buried in two books when this one came along, but all three were in on time, so something went right. I'd like to add a personal thank you to Gary, Dave, Jacob, Jason, Liz, Maya, Ralph and Richard at Disinformation for everything – this is what we wanted, and this is what you got.

The impact that Monty Python has had around the world is incredible. To date, you can buy every episode of the cult classic TV show on DVD, but only in America! You might like to own a *Monty Python London A-Z Street Guide*, but the drawback is that it's written in Japanese! In England, their country of origin, we've got some catching up to do, but hopefully this volume will give some insight into what might be possible in the future. Man and boy, I've been a Monty Python fan – more recently, I was given the chance to work with them on their entire CD back catalogue, a genuine dream come true. Gentlemen, I salute you – the entire trip has been a pleasure.

Alan Parker
(Not expecting a Spanish Inquisition in Maida Vale, London.)

INTRODUCTION: BUT! COMPLETELY DIFFERENT

What do I have in common with the late, great George Harrison? Well, just like the ex-Beatle, I was called in at the eleventh hour to help out on a Monty Python project – but whereas George was on hand to provide financial backing in order to rescue *Life of Brian* from financial collapse, I was called upon by Alan to assist him with the text for the book you're about to read, and hopefully enjoy.

I will readily admit to the fact that, unlike Alan, who is Python-mad and possesses a sizeable collection ranging from books, a board game, DVDs and many framed things, to a bizarre and somewhat disturbing set of *Holy Grail* Python action men, I, apart from believing *Life of Brian* to be one of the best movies ever made, had little more than a layman's appreciation for the good ship Monty Python, and the six lunatics that were manning her sails. I was barely into my teens when the fourth, and final, *Monty Python's Flying Circus* series came to an end some time in 1974. (And yes, before all you Python anoraks go getting your Gumbies in a twist, I do know the final series' title was truncated to plain old *Monty Python* in recognition of John Cleese's departure from the team after the third series.)

I do remember, however, seeing the occasional episode when the show was first broadcast on TV, which was a result of my Dad being something of a Python fan, but the Oxbridge boys' unique fusion of intellectual, satirical and observational humour was completely off the comedic chart as far as I was concerned. And though I thoroughly enjoyed watching *Holy Grail* at the cinema, and also the by-then-defunct team's solo projects such as Cleese's *Fawlty Towers*, Palin's *Ripping Yarns* and, to a lesser degree, Idle's *Rutland Weekend Television*, it wasn't until some five years later when the MPFC shows were repeated by the BBC that I finally gained some appreciation of the Python team's incredible collective talent.

I would like to thank the following people, places and institutions for helping keep me sane during the writing of this and my other books: Alan Parker, for having invited me on to this project when there were many others equally suited to the task, and for countless other things too numerous to mention – thanks again, mate. Paul Young (not the singer, I hasten to add), who can, and does on many an occasion, effortlessly rhyme off the dialogue from various Python sketches. Jake, Bruce, Ian and Steve, collectively known as Stiff Little Fingers, and still burning some twenty-nine years after the flame was first ignited. Angela, the 'angel of NYC'; Sid n' Oscar; Mum & Dad; the boys from the Los Angeles Glasgow Rangers Supporters Club, who recently went that extra mile to make this humble (non-practicing) Catholic boy feel welcome; the 'Two Toms'; Gary at Disinformation; and Sean and Graham at Helter Skelter Publishing.

Yet again, and probably not for the last time, I would like to take time out to thank my wife Jakki, for her patience, encouragement and for never once complaining about being sidelined in favour of 'Monty' – a man she's never even met!

Mick O'Shea

CHAPTER ONE: GROUNDBREAKING TELEVISION

Gilliam is one of the most manipulative bastards in that group of utterly manipulative bastards. Michael is a selfish bastard, Cleese a control freak, Jonesy is shagged out and now forgets everything, and Graham, as you know, is still dead. I'm the only really nice one! (Eric Idle)

In the beginning, there were six guys. Michael Palin was studying history at Oxford along with Terry Jones, who was studying English. Over at Cambridge, John Cleese was studying law (by his own admission, Cleese had no plans on comedy as a career move – in fact, he always thought he was going to be a lawyer, and when he did turn to showbiz he was incredibly naïve). Meanwhile, Eric Idle was studying English and Graham Chapman had chosen medicine – a fact that, years later, would shock the living daylights out of frequent Python collaborator Neil Innes when he fell ill at the Hollywood Bowl and it was Chapman who wrote his prescription. Over in the US, a young Terry Gilliam was studying political science in Los Angeles.

Our only aim was to be as funny as we could possibly be. We just wanted to make people laugh as much as we could force them to. (John Cleese)

While they had all been greatly impressed by comedy, most notably *The Goon Show* (a surreal, satirical and highly influential radio series that ran throughout the 1950s, created by Spike Milligan and also written by Peter Sellers, Harry Secombe, Michael Bentine and Eric

Cambridge Footlights

Cambridge University Footlights Dramatic Club, commonly referred to simply as the Footlights, is an amateur theatrical club in Cambridge, England, run by the students of Cambridge University and now also the Anglia Ruskin University (formerly Anglia Polytechnic University). It was founded in 1883.

It grew in prominence in the 1960s, as a hotbed of comedy and satire, and continues to produce the regular (and very popular) *Smokers* at the ADC Theatre, including informal mixtures of sketches and stand-up.

Notable entertainers who were members, or who worked with, the Footlights include Douglas Adams (author of *The Hitchhiker's Guide to the Galaxy*), Sacha Baron Cohen (Ali G), actors Stephen Fry and Hugh Laurie, feminist author Germaine Greer and actress Emma Thompson.

Pythons Graham Chapman, John Cleese and Eric Idle were all members.

– From Wikipedia.com

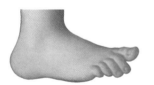

Trivia Fact: The first time Monty Python was written about by *Radio Times*, the BBC's weekly programme listings magazine, it was under the headline 'Will Monty Python Collect £200?' This was, of course, a reference to the Monopoly board game rule that if you pass 'Go', you collect £200.

Sykes) none of them had thought about a career in this field until they became aware of *Beyond the Fringe*, which starred the influential, anti-establishment satirist Peter Cook, and proved that ex-Cambridge Footlights people could actually get paid for doing this kind of thing. (*Beyond the Fringe* was a stage show that combined the best of the Cambridge Footlights and Oxford Revue's Edinburgh runs, which went on to become a smash hit in London and New York, and is often credited as an inspiration for the English satire boom of the 1960s.)

Terry Jones left college to start as a script advisor at BBC TV in the comedy department. His jobs included writing potential filler material for, among others, the comedian Ken Dodd and pianist Russ Conway. After a short time he got Michael Palin involved, and they made their TV debut together as extras on *The Ken Dodd Show* in a sketch about tramps. Thus (pretty much overnight) a writing team was born. They continued to write for *The Billy Cotton Band Show* on radio, pop star Kathy Kirby and, to be honest, anybody they could sell material to. It was David Frost, presenter of the satirical news programme *That Was the Week That Was*, and another Footlights alum, who effectively discovered Palin and landed him the incredibly cushy job of presenting the 1966 TV pop show *Now!*, providing him with a salary of £35 for one day's work a week (almost unheard of in 1966). This meant that he could live fairly comfortably while still working with Terry Jones on new ideas.

Michael talks a lot. Yap yap yap he goes, all day long and through the night, twenty-three to the dozen, the ground littered with hind legs of donkeys, till you believe it is not possible for him to go on any longer, but he does. He must be the worst man in the world to take on a commando raid. (John Cleese)

Volatile, dominant, highly energised, svelte, acerbic and coruscating are all words that Terry Jones uses with uncertainty. (John Cleese)

John Cleese and Graham Chapman went to New York in 1965 with the Cambridge Footlights troupe. While there, Cleese met Terry Gilliam, then an editor (along with Gloria Steinem) of ex-*Mad* cartoonist Harvey Kurtzman's crazy and rather close-to-the-edge *Help!* magazine. One of the common features in the magazine was the photo story, with a comic assembled from photos captioned with speech bubbles. While in Manhattan, Cleese agreed to star in the story of a man who falls in love with his daughter's Barbie doll, and then consummates the relationship (Woody Allen and Orson Bean had also appeared in photo stories for the magazine). Gilliam and Cleese became friends on the spot, exchanging telephone numbers before Cleese headed home to the UK. Meanwhile, David Frost, another Cambridge old boy, had launched a very successful comedy career with the BBC – his second production, *The Frost Report* (the successor to *That Was the Week That Was*), featured the recently-recruited John Cleese and Graham Chapman, who would also contribute as a writing team. The show soon turned Cleese into a star – by the time Michael Palin had heard of him, he was already commanding near-legendary status among his peers. This show also introduced the public to the comic duo of Ronnie Barker and Ronnie Corbet, who would later bring an audience of 22 million to Saturday nights on BBC television, under their collective working name *The Two Ronnies* (a programme that would include sketches by Palin and Jones). Additional material written by the fast-rising team of Palin and Jones was bought for the show, but *The Frost Report* didn't exactly pay big money. Newcomer Eric Idle, all of twenty-three years of age, also contributed – this must certainly be the first genuine Python collaboration.

Some friends call Gilliam a Renaissance man; others place him earlier. The sloping forehead, the forward slant of the body as he lopes, and the prognathous jaw all point to the Upper Paleolithic period. (John Cleese)

David Frost was asked by the BBC to produce another series. *At Last the 1948 Show* (the title was a reference to the agonizing amount of time that the BBC would often leave new shows on the shelf for) would be a landmark, and set the stage for *Monty Python's Flying Circus* to debut two years later. John Cleese would star, along with Graham Chapman, Tim Brooke-Taylor, Marty Feldman and Amy Macdonald. The last sketch in the first episode of *1948* was an early version of future Python sketch 'Four Yorkshiremen', played out at this time by Cleese and Chapman, with Tim Brooke-Taylor and Marty Feldman. At roughly the same time that the BBC were transmitting *1948*, ITV launched *Do Not Adjust Your Set*, a new kids' programme. It was shown at 5.25pm – the teatime market. The bunch of young people responsible for the show didn't really seem to pay this fact much attention, and just carried on writing their own material and amusing themselves. This new show starred Eric Idle, Terry Jones, Michael Palin, David Jason and Denise Coffey, a team that would soon be joined by a wacky, mad-cap animator from the US named Terry Gilliam who, having just hitch-hiked his way around Europe, phoned Cleese and got some contact numbers. He turned up in a big fur coat with a beautiful, model-looking girlfriend, and although he started by

Satire Boom

The 'satire boom' is a general term used to describe the emergence of a generation of English satirical writers, journalists and performers at the end of the 1950s. The figures most closely identified with it are Peter Cook, John Bird, John Fortune, David Frost, Bernard Levin and Richard Ingrams. Many of the figures who found initial celebrity through the satire boom went on to subsequently establish more serious careers as writers, including Alan Bennett (drama), Jonathan Miller (polymathic), Paul Foot (investigative journalism) and Germaine Greer (academic feminism).

In his book *The Neophiliacs*, Christopher Booker, who as founding editor of *Private Eye* magazine was a central figure of the satire boom, charts the years 1959 to 1964. He begins with the Cambridge Footlights student revue *The Last Laugh*, written by Bird and Cook. It transferred to a West End theatre. Booker ends the period with the cancellation of the television series *That Was the Week That Was*, and the closing of the Establishment Club in Soho, Peter Cook's showcase for many of the leading lights of the movement.

The boom was driven by well-connected graduates from, first, the University of Cambridge, and then the University of Oxford. Booker argues that, with the response to the Suez Crisis which effectively marked the end of the British Empire as a great power, an upper middle class generation with public school and Oxbridge educations who had grown up with certain expectations – of following a career in colonial administration or the civil service – suddenly found themselves surplus. Peter Cook had already entered for a Foreign Office entrance exam, before his stage career took off. The satire boom generation were in general apolitical or had (at that time) left-of-centre tendencies.

– From Wikipedia.com

At Last the 1948 Show

At Last the 1948 Show was made shortly before the introduction of colour on ITV. There were two short series totalling thirteen twenty-five minute episodes (six episodes in the first series, and seven episodes in the second series). Some time later Paradine Productions decided to wipe the series, and eleven out of the thirteen episodes of the series were destroyed. Much of the missing material still exists in the form of audio recordings from the series or from the LP version, and the surviving video footage has reportedly been restored by the British Film Institute.

Some surviving sketches from *At Last the 1948 Show* have now been released on DVD, including the 'Four Yorkshiremen' sketch with the original cast of John Cleese, Graham Chapman, Tim Brooke-Taylor and Marty Feldman.

– From Wikipedia.com

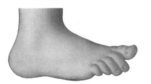

Trivia Fact: When Monty Python first appeared in the *Radio Times* TV listings, for the first episode of the show in October 1969, it was under a very large picture of Carol Cleveland.

selling sketches, it was his soon-to-be-famous animation that stole the show. *Do Not Adjust Your Set* also featured the Bonzo Dog Doo-Dah Band, whose line-up included a young Neil Innes.

After the first series was transmitted, Thames TV decided their new young talent was good enough to offer them a genuine night time forty-five minute comedy show, but the offer came at a price – there would be no spare sound stages to film on for eighteen months! While this most bizarre of offers was still sinking in, a call came from John Cleese and Graham Chapman, to see if the *Do Not* team would like to work with them. **Cleese and Chapman had realized that they now both came as part of a team.**

Marty Feldman and I were sitting in an Indian restaurant. He had been working on The Frost Report *with John and Graham, and I'd been working at Thames Television with Michael and Terry J., and I said, "I'll put my two Oxford chaps against your two Cambridge chaps." It started as a joke – hah hah hah – so I got home and I thought, "Hey, that's not a bad idea." So I put it to Michael, and he said yeah, he thought it'd be fine by him, but if it came off could he bring Eric and Terry G. because they'd been working together at Thames. And I took it to John and Graham, and we got together and talked about it, and I went to the BBC.*
(Barry Took)

One can only imagine what kind of magic Barry Took, the BBC comedy advisor who had brought together the future Pythons from the ranks of *At Last the 1948 Show* and *Do Not Adjust Your Set*, weaved when he talked about these boys, because what follows you really couldn't make up. They were invited in for an interview with Michael Mills (head of comedy at BBC), and for his part Mills asked all the usual questions: What are you going to call the show? Will it have musical guests? Will there be guest stars? In answer to all of these questions the future Pythons answered, simply, "We don't know!" The answer they were given was a most bizarre "Alright, I'll give you 13 shows, but that's it".

UN-USED TV SHOW NAMES:
'The Amazing Flying Circus'
'Arthur Buzzard's Flying School'
'Arthur Megapode's Cheap Show'
'Arthur Megapode's Flying Circus'
'Baron Von Took's Flying Circus'
'Bob Python's Flying Circus'
'Brian's Flying Circus'
'Bum, Wackett, Buzzard, Stubble & Boot'
'The Comedy Zoo'
'Cynthia Fellatio's Flying Circus'
'The Down Show'
'Gwen Dibley's Flying Circus'
'The Horrible Earnest Megapode'
'A Horse, a Spoon & a Basin'
'The Joke Zoo'
'The Laughing Zoo'
'Man's Crisis of Identity in the Latter Half of the Twentieth Century'
'Megapode's Cheap Show'
'O'
'123'
'Ow! It's Colin Plint!'
'Owl Stretching Time'
'The Panic Show'
'The People Zoo'
'The Plastic Mac Show'
'A Spoon & a Basin'
'A Toad Elevating Moment'
'Vaseline Parade'
'The Year of the Stoat'
'Zoo Show!'

Do Not Adjust Your Set

Series one of *Do Not Adjust Your Set* consisted of fourteen episodes of thirty minutes, broadcast between 26 December 1967 and 28 March 1968, Thursdays at 5.25pm. Series two consisted of thirteen episodes of thirty minutes broadcast between 19 February 1969 and 14 May 1969, Wednesdays at 5.20pm. Specials included an untitled show of thirty minutes broadcast 29 July 1968, Monday at 7pm; and *Do Not Adjust Your Stocking*, fifty minutes, broadcast 25 December 1968, Wednesday at 4.10pm.

In common with *At Last the 1948 Show*, many episodes were wiped despite their importance to the history of British television comedy, and the surviving episodes are seldom repeated.

Nine of the fourteen episodes from the first (Rediffusion) series (presumably all that survive) were released on DVD in the UK and the US by August 2005. Both releases use the same NTSC Region 0 discs made from telerecordings of the original videotapes. The packaging claims that Gilliam's animations appear in these episodes, but they do not.

— From Wikipedia.com

By then I had become the advisor to the comedy department at the BBC on what they called cheerfully a 'peppercorn rent', meaning they paid me nothing but I was allowed to steal; I didn't steal because I'm not that sort of person, but I desperately wanted to get some shows together. (Barry Took)

Pretty soon after we decided to do something together, John and Graham went off to finish a film they were doing with Carlo Ponti or somebody like that and then take a holiday in Ibiza, leaving Terry and myself and Terry Gilliam to think more about a shape for the show. That would have happened during May or June 1969; when they came back we actually started writing. (Michael Palin)

Carol Cleveland

Carol Cleveland is a British comic actress, most notable for her appearances as the only significant female performer in *Monty Python's Flying Circus*. She also appeared with Spike Milligan and on *The Benny Hill Show*, *The Two Ronnies* and other TV shows and films. She appeared in all four seasons of *Flying Circus* and all five of the Monty Python movies. Privately called Carol Cleavage by the other Pythons, Carol played a caricature of the blonde bombshell stereotype. Stage directions for her first sketch described her as 'a blonde buxom wench in the full bloom of womanhood'. Although she did not really enjoy being restricted this way, her performances were brilliant and hilarious. She called herself the 'glamour stooge'.

She is a former Miss California Navy and appeared as Miss Teen Queen in *Mad* magazine at age fifteen. She also studied at the Royal Academy of Dramatic Art and now performs in a one-woman show, *Carol Cleveland Reveals All*.

Her mother, known as Pat, appeared in *Monty Python* on several occasions, once as a mental patient with an axe embedded in her head.

– From Wikipedia.com

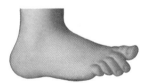

Trivia Fact: John Cleese, as a child, was often tormented because of his height (he was 6'3" by the age of twelve) but was able to use his talent for humour as a means of deflecting aggressive behaviour from his peers.

I remember sitting on the grass in some London park idly discussing what we should do. Me, Mike, Terry G. and Terry J. already had an offer to do an adult version of Do Not Adjust Your Set *on ITV, but not for another year. John and Graham came with an offer to go straight ahead in the autumn. John was keen to get Mike, and we had him; therefore he came with us.* (Eric Idle)

With their commission in place, the six of them began writing. All was going very well over at Terry Jones' house when suddenly, without any warning, the BBC transmitted *Q5*, the latest series from Spike Milligan. It quite simply changed all the rules in the comedy handbook. Sketches no longer needed punch lines; guests were, if need be, a thing of the past. The team did some soul-searching before continuing with their work. One of the original ideas had been that all the female roles would be played by the team themselves, something they pretty much stuck to for old ladies and eccentric dames. These characters later became known in Python language as 'pepper-pots', but it was equally obvious that they would need a real female lead. After all, some sketches required genuine glamour, and for this they turned to TV actress Carol Cleveland, who had already chalked up some success with appearances in *The Avengers* and *The Saint*. The proposed series had its players, and its content, and an instantly identifiable theme tune in the form of John Philip Sousa's 'Liberty Bell March', but before it could be put out on air it would also need a name. The team came up with several suggestions, including 'Owl-Stretching Time', 'Bum, Wackett, Buzzard, Stubble & Boot' and 'A Horse, a Spoon & a Basin', before finally deciding upon 'Flying Circus'. As Cleese says in the blurb accompanying the 2002 DVD release of *And Now for Something Completely Different*, although everyone was in favour of 'Flying Circus', the 'circus' was in need of an owner, and as all six were vehemently against using one of their names like so many other humdrum shows, they decided upon a fictitious name. 'Monty Python' was chosen as 'Monty' conjured up connotations of people with seedy little moustaches, pretending that they'd had something to do with the war in the African desert ('Monty' was the nickname for First Viscount Bernard Law Montgomery, who had achieved lasting fame for having led the British Eighth Army to victory against Rommel, at El Alamein during World War II), and 'Python' conjured up images of treacherous theatrical and musical agent types. *Monty Python's Flying Circus* was first broadcast on BBC 1 at 10.55pm on 5 October 1969 – but you could hardly call it a runaway success. The studio audience barely laughed at the first episode. By the end of the first series, the show had a constantly shifting time spot, and could

Monty Python, The Early Years (from left to right): Terry Jones, Graham Chapman, John Cleese, Eric Idle, Terry Gilliam and Michael Palin.

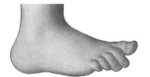

be cancelled at the blink of an eye if anything more important came along – and at the BBC of the 1960s, 'more important' might include anything from the cricket running over to the worry of having the snooker running over on the other side!

I remember after, in the bar, certain people who were quite close friends saying, "Oh well, no, won't have a drink tonight, got to dash off home, you know, the babysitters" – they didn't even have babies! (Michael Palin)

Despite these initial teething problems, the series had tripled its audience to an impressive three million viewers by the end of the first run. By the time of the second series, the BBC had not only increased the show's budget, but far more importantly, it had also guaranteed the show a regular time slot. *Monty Python* quickly became a comedy classic.

Over the course of four years the team produced forty-five episodes of the hit TV show (which are now available in the US as a sixteen-DVD box set, while at home in the UK, the birthplace of Python, there is a single DVD 'Best of' to spotlight their collective genius, which only goes to prove that rarely is a prophet recognised in his or her own land). Thirty-nine of these included John Cleese, who made the decision to walk away after three series. By Cleese's own admission, he'd said "let's work together", not "let's get married!"

Trivia Fact: The first series of *Monty Python's Flying Circus* was originally broadcast in the UK from 5 October 1969 to 11 January 1970, the second from 15 September 1970 to 22 December 1970 and the third from 19 October 1972 to 18 January 1973. The fourth series, simply called *Monty Python*, ran from 31 October 1974 to 5 December 1974.

Trivia Fact: Inspired by Spike Milligan's *Q5*, the Monty Python team decided to take the still-risky move of not using punch lines in the show. This is spoofed in the 'Restaurant' sketch. They also pioneered the 'cold intro', where the shows began without opening credits.

Cleese departed to concentrate on writing what would become the first series of *Fawlty Towers*, and in recognition of this significant loss, the rest of the team decided to drop 'Flying Circus' from the series' name and went out instead as plain old *Monty Python*. It also soon became public knowledge that Cleese's writing partner Graham Chapman was an alcoholic, and was becoming almost impossible to work with. Having lost Cleese, the team completed one more series, but in this instance the series contained just six episodes, not the previous thirteen. Cleese, however, would receive an onscreen writing credit on the last six, which also included more guest appearances, due to a larger budget. The most notable new face on screen was the American writer and actress Connie Booth (who was, of course, Mrs John Cleese at the time).

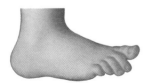

Trivia Fact: While the A&E DVD releases of *Monty Python's Flying Circus* contain the uncut versions of each episode, they also exclude some details, including some dialogue from the 'Biggles Dictates a Letter' sketch, Graham Chapman singing 'Tonight Tonight' in the 'Funny Bus Conductor' sketch, the 'Dad's Pooves' film which originally ran at the end of episode thirty-eight and the word 'masturbation' in the 'All-England Summarize Proust Competition' sketch. It also includes a different version of the musical intro to the Arthur 'Two Sheds' Jackson interview than originally broadcast.

The Pythons had been doing location work in Torquay, and had stayed at the Gleneagles Hotel, run by a Mr Donald Sinclair, who John Cleese would later describe as the rudest man ever! Unknown to him, Sinclair was later to be the inspiration for *Fawlty Towers*, John and Connie's first collaboration. Basil Fawlty was Sinclair to a tee. In a later BBC interview, Cleese pointed out that Eric Idle had left his briefcase in reception one morning. On arriving back that night Idle asked if his case had been seen, only to be informed by Sinclair that it was across the wrong side of the hotel swimming pool behind a wall; not unnaturally, Idle wondered why behind the desk in reception wasn't good enough, only to be told, "Well, we sacked someone recently, it might have been a bomb!" By the end of their stay in Torquay every member of the Python team had checked out of the Gleneagles, apart from Cleese.

In the years beyond their small screen success the group would hit the big screen four times, produce eight original albums for Charisma Records (these will be expanded with bonus tracks and re-issued by EMI/Capitol Records in 2006, along with a new totally un-issued Python album) and go on to achieve a wagonload of solo success.

I feel that we changed the Twentieth Century. The atom bomb, the Russians' success at Stalingrad, the information revolution and probably the 1953 Cup Final would not have been possible without Monty Python! (John Cleese)

Rumours of a full Python reunion would linger throughout the Eighties. By the summer of 1988, Graham Chapman had just completed a US-based comedy show titled *Jake's Journey*, which he wrote and starred in. He had worked as executive producer on the movie *Love Potion* and recently gone back to an old script titled *Ditto*, which he'd collaborated on with John Cleese some twenty years earlier. His tour of universities in the US, where he basically sat chatting to students and answering questions, was issued by Rykodisc (RDVD10/503) under the title *Looks Like a Brown Trouser Job* in 2005, and while it's made up of totally hand-filmed home video footage, it does contain some hysterical footage covering topics from the Dangerous Sports Club to life as a mate of The Who's Keith Moon. In November he made a visit to his doctor, who found a growth on his tonsils. It was immediately diagnosed as throat cancer, and in no time the disease had spread to his spine. Despite difficult and painful surgery, Graham continued to work. In the New Year of 1989 he contributed to *Parrot Sketch Not Included* (a new Python documentary), *The Movie Life of George* (a documentary on Handmade Films) and took a small roll in the Iron Maiden promo video for 'Can I Play With Madness'. However, in September 1989 he was rushed to hospital, where doctors pronounced his cancer incurable. Family and friends rushed to his side, but Graham lost his battle on October 4. Both Michael Palin and John Cleese were at his side. The following day was, of course, planned to celebrate twenty years since the first broadcast of Monty Python, but Graham's death meant the party had to be postponed. "It was," claimed Terry Jones, "the worst case of party-pooping I've ever seen."

The Monty Python team did not attend Graham's funeral by choice; they voted to make that a private day for David Sherlock (Graham's partner) and Graham's family, instead of the media circus that their presence would have assured. They did send a wreath, a large Python-style foot bearing the words: "To Graham from the other Pythons. Stop us if we're getting too silly." Two months after Graham's death, the team held a service of its own at St Bart's Hospital Great Hall. Eric led the gathered crowd in a rousing chorus of 'Always Look on the Bright Side of Life,' while John Cleese later addressed the congregation, "Graham Chapman is no more. He has gone to meet his maker. He has run down the curtain and joined the choir invisible," before becoming the first human being on the planet to utter the word 'fuck' at a memorial service. All of the team and a number of old friends from British comedy contributed. Eric Idle later fought back the tears while telling everyone that Graham had always thought Michael Palin talked way too much, and had obviously decided to die rather than listen to him anymore.

Connie Booth

Connie Booth (born 1944 in Indianapolis, Indiana, USA) is an American writer and actress best known for her appearances on British television, especially her work with her ex-husband, John Cleese.

She made her first appearance on British television in 1968. She appeared regularly in *Monty Python's Flying Circus*. She also appeared in *Monty Python and the Holy Grail* as the woman accused of being a witch. She co-wrote and co-starred (as the maid, Polly) in the series *Fawlty Towers* with her then-husband, John Cleese.

Booth and Cleese were married from 15 February 1968 to 1978 when their marriage ended in divorce. They had one child, Cynthia Cleese (born 1971), from their decade-long marriage.

Connie Booth subsequently appeared in dramatic roles on British television and her ability to switch back to her American accent proved useful in several roles, including Mrs Errol in a BBC adaptation of *Little Lord Fauntleroy* and Miss March in a dramatisation of Edith Wharton's *The Buccaneers*.

She ended her acting career and now practices as a psychotherapist in London.

– *From Wikipedia.com*

THE ORIGIN OF THE FOOT

Many Python sketches were linked together by the often-hilarious cut-out animations of Terry Gilliam, including the opening titles featuring the iconic giant foot that became a symbol of all that was "Python-esque." Gilliam's unique visual style was characterized by sudden and dramatic movements and errors of scale set in surrealist landscapes populated by engravings of large buldings with elaborate architecture, grotesque victorian gadgets, machinery, and people cut from old Sears Roebuck catalogs, supported by Gilliam's airbrush illustrations and many famous pieces of art. All of these elements were combined in incongruous ways to obtain new and humourous meanings in the tradition of surrealist collage assemblies. The giant foot is appropriated from the figure of Cupid in Agnolo Bronzino's *An Allegory of Venus and Cupid*.

– *From Wikipedia.com*

CHAPTER TWO: MATCHING TIE AND HANDKERCHIEF

Rock fame is a funny old thing. Sure, you can make money out of garbage or twenty-four carat gold, but it is given only to the very few to manage to do both at the same time! (Meatloaf, in the *Spam to Sperm* documentary)

For a long time I thought they were a record act. I had no idea they did a TV show. (Steve Martin)

When *Monty Python's Flying Circus* began as a TV show in 1969, it was without a musical section. The way that pretty much all television stations commissioned comedy or light entertainment at the time, however, was to include some sort of musical guest spot, or a musical section provided by the cast of the show itself. The only music linked to Python's earliest days was 'Liberty Bell' and that, according to Terry Gilliam, was chosen from a number of recordings brought in by one of the show's production team.

Rather like the title Monty Python's Flying Circus, *which meant nothing, we wanted music that meant nothing and didn't give any clue as to what it was going to be like, and it was desperately important that it wasn't comedy music, so we went for something completely against type.* (Michael Palin on 'Liberty Bell')

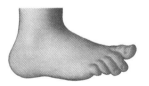

Trivia Fact: *Monty Python's Flying Circus* **was ranked #5 in the 30 May 2004 TV *Guide's* list of the '25 Top Cult Shows Ever'.**

Neil Innes

Neil Innes is a writer and performer of comic songs, best known for playing in the Bonzo Dog Doo-Dah Band and, later, the Rutles.

In the period 1962 to 1965, Innes and several other art school students started a band, which was originally named the Bonzo Dog Dada Band after their interest in the art movement Dada, but which was soon renamed the Bonzo Dog Doo-Dah Band (often shortened to the Bonzo Dog Band). Innes, with Vivian Stanshall, wrote most of the band's songs, including 'I'm the Urban Spaceman', their sole hit, and 'Death Cab for Cutie' (which inspired an American musical group of the same name), which was featured in the Beatles' film *Magical Mystery Tour*.

In the 1970s, Innes joined with Eric Idle to create the television comedy series *Rutland Weekend Television*. This show spawned the Rutles (the 'prefab four'), a Beatles parody band, in which Innes played the character of Ron Nasty, loosely based on John Lennon. Innes also played Nasty in *All You Need Is Cash*.

It would be the last item of the second series that would open up a whole new avenue for the talent of this groundbreaking comedy team. A sketch that felt like it was going nowhere really had to find an ending somehow. The decision was made to end with a song named, rather bizarrely, 'Spam'.

We did use music when sketches had run their normal course, and had nowhere else to go; 'Spam' is a wonderful example. (Michael Palin)

It's just stupid, there's no reason for anything. Why are the Vikings there? Why are they dressed as Vikings? Why are they singing love songs to pressed meat? (Eric Idle)

Years ago — I think it was after the second series of Python — I was with my wife in Greece, and we were travelling around with a little tent, and woke up one morning hearing people in a neighbouring tent singing 'spam, spam, spam', so it started fairly early on, these songs spreading. (Terry Gilliam)

With one number already under their collective belts, the Pythons decided to soldier on in the same vein, even though it had already occurred to them that if they were completely honest they only really had one potential singer in a group made up of six!

I think we were all a bit nervous about doing this kind of thing originally. I certainly remember being very nervous about singing in the TV studio. (Terry Jones)

All of us within the group enjoyed music and songs, and most of us at the time were tone deaf. (Michael Palin)

Eric actually had a decent voice. Terry Jones, oh dear, well, it was all right if it was a Welsh song I suppose, very loud and ruckus and over the top. Terry Gilliam, oh, sing! (Carol Cleveland)

Graham used to howl beautifully, "Oooh..." [makes the sound of a Python 'pepper pot' lady], if indeed that is of musical importance. John is absolutely useless. (Terry Gilliam)

I'm probably the worst singer in Europe! I won't compete for North America, I always have been. I was kicked out of singing lessons by Mr Hickley to do extra Greek! (John Cleese)

The Pythons having a good laugh (from left to right): Eric Idle, Graham Chapman, Michael Palin, John Cleese, Terry Jones, Terry Gilliam.

John is not very comfortable singing, I don't think. I don't think he's very comfortable with music. (Michael Palin)

Of course, by the time they were making their hit films and appearing on stage, the team had been fleshed out by the inclusion of ex-Bonzo Dog Doo-Dah Band member Neil Innes, but before the former Sixties pop star was even involved with Python they continued on their path of song writing. What they came up with next provided them with not only a hit single, but also an everlasting cult classic...

Michael and I had been writing on the day about a barber, this psychotic barber, snip-snip-snip, and we couldn't think of a way of getting out or finishing it. (Terry Jones)

I think one of us must have just said, why doesn't he just say "I didn't want to be a barber anyway, I wanted to be a lumberjack," and it just came out almost as it is now. By quarter past seven we'd written it down and we were in the pub having a pint. (Michael Palin)

I've also sung it in German which was quite extraordinary, because we did a show in Germany. (Michael Palin)

Innes also contributed to the Pythons' final BBC TV series in 1974 – he wrote a squib of a song called 'George III' (sung by a pastiche black American girl group), which appears in the episode 'The Golden Age of Ballooning'. He wrote the song 'Where Does a Dream Begin?' (included in the episode 'Anything Goes: The Light Entertainment War'), and he co-wrote the 'Most Awful Family in Britain' sketch in the last episode, 'Party Political Broadcast'. He is one of only two non-Pythons to ever be credited as a writer for the TV series, the other one being Douglas Adams (who co-wrote another sketch in 'Party Political Broadcast', in which a patient profusely bleeding from the stomach is made to sign numerous senseless forms before being treated).

Innes appeared in *Monty Python and the Holy Grail*, playing a head-bashing monk and the leader of Sir Robin's minstrels, and in Terry Gilliam's *Jabberwocky*. He also appeared with the Pythons at their legendary Hollywood Bowl concert. Because of these long-standing connections, Innes is often referred to as 'the Seventh Python'.

– From Wikipedia.com

Michael inadvertently came out and it was hilarious, we were actually cracking up, because he looked like Hitler, and there's Hitler singing... (Eric Idle)

A record deal for Python albums and singles came about via the Charisma Records label. At the time, the label was best known as the home of rock band Genesis, who were committed Python fans (they would later help finance *Holy Grail*). During their time with Charisma, the Python team produced eight albums (see Appendix Three for further information). Believe it or not, the recording career that would give them rock star status started out in a little garden shed.

The first album was done in Andre Jacquemin's parents' garden shed... at the end of the garden was a little shed and Andre converted it into a tiny little studio. You had to crouch when you went in there. (Terry Gilliam)

Andre's mother, who was wonderful at baking cakes, would keep bringing us cakes all the time, so we'd just sit there and munch cakes and do a little recording, and look at the goldfish pond. (Michael Palin)

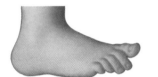

Trivia Fact: The term 'spam', as used to denote unsolicited e-mail, comes from Monty Python's 'Spam' sketch. The Hormel Company, which produces Spam, has been very good-natured about the infamous song and only requires that unwanted junk mail be referred to with a lower-case 's'.
– From Wikipedia.com

What would happen is that each of them individually, if they'd written a song, they would all have their tiny cassette recorders and sing into them. It was really then that the hard work started off, actually putting it all together to decipher the meaning of their melodies and things. (Andre Jacquemin)

The next song they came up with would also give them another UK chart placing and hit single status. This time the subject matter was so off-the-wall as to only be really possible in Pythonland. It dealt with an insect that was only half present...

'Eric the Half-a-Bee' was written on location in Germany, outside Munich where we were filming with John Cleese, and John was dressed as Little Red Riding Hood, which is unforgettable if you've never seen John dressed in Bavarian drag! (Eric Idle)

Eric and I had just started to ad-lib a little bit together, and my recollection is that the song began to come out of that, but it's actually one of my absolute favourites. (John Cleese)

The continued release of successful albums and spin-off singles only made Python's rock star status more concrete. Some of the biggest rock groups in the world were fans, and rumour had it that some groups (Pink Floyd being a notable example) actually organised recording sessions and their gigs around the screening of Python TV shows. The team's own brushes with their newfound star status actually began on their first stage tour, in Canada.

We did a rather hit-and-miss Python tour of Canada in the early Seventies. It was the first time we ever went abroad on stage with Python, and we got to Vancouver and just had to hum the Lumberjack song. Didn't have to sing a word. And they went berserk. (Michael Palin)

In New York at the City Center, which is the first time we knew that Python was big there, we came out of the stage door after the first night's show, and as we came out the door there were 200 screaming fans, and I remember this one girl throwing herself at Michael, and swooning in his arms. (Carol Cleveland)

There was something about what we were doing, I guess, that was anarchic and was touching rock n' roll sensibilities, and anti-authoritarian sensibilities, and we were the comic voice for that at the moment, and so we got the benefit of being treated like rock n' roll stars, which was fantastic. (Terry Gilliam)

By 1980, with all but one of their albums released, and having seen both *Holy Grail* and *Life of Brian* fill cinemas across the globe, the Python team was in a position to sell out the famous Hollywood Bowl for four nights, playing to eight thousand people. They had now conquered both small and large screens, the pop charts and the live stage. Their collective path was blocked by nothing.

They would have had a good time if we'd just done the phone book, I think. I mean, they were determined to have a good time. I think we did four days, it was just great. (Eric Idle)

It was a lovely balmy evening, there was a lovely feeling of freedom about it, and the crowds were so friendly. (John Cleese)

The eight Python albums were first issued on CD in the late '80s via Virgin Records, on their 'Blah Blah Blah' comedy offshoot label. This continued to be their official format until 2006, when a new batch of better pressings, all featuring additional material, was made available by EMI Records (the full story of the quest to re-release this material can be found in this book's afterword).

Trivia Fact: *Matching Tie & Handkerchief* was billed as the world's first three-sided record, with a second groove cut into the second side. Different material could be heard depending on which groove the needle was placed in.

Trivia Fact: *Monty Python's Instant Record Collection* was originally packaged with a fold-out cover which simulated a stack of records. This kept breaking in stores and was eventually replaced with a simpler version.

CHAPTER THREE:
AND NOW FOR SOMETHING
COMPLETELY DIFFERENT

Oh, I'm a lumberjack and I'm okay,
I sleep all night and I work all day,
I chop down trees,
I wear high heels,
Suspenders and a bra,
I wish I'd been a girlie,
Just like my dear papa...

And Now for Something Completely Different, which was directed by Ian MacNaughton (who directed all but the first four *Python* episodes, and also made a cameo appearance in the movie) and produced by Patricia Casey, opened to general cinema release in September 1971, and saw the Python team successfully making the decidedly risky transition from terrestrial television to the 'big screen'.

The idea for the movie came about as a means of introducing the show to American audiences, as the Python team was convinced that their special brand of humour would go down well on the US college circuit. The movie therefore consisted of an anthology of the team's best sketches taken from the first two series of *Monty Python's Flying Circus*; with the TV show's opening salutation being chosen as the title. The filming, which cost an estimated £80,000, took place over an eight-week period during November – December 1970, with most of the interior scenes being shot in a disused milk depot in north London. The movie opened in London on 28 September 1971, and although it quickly recouped its production costs, it failed to make any significant impact upon its release in America the following August. It wouldn't be until the autumn of 1974, when the PBS network began regularly broadcasting the *Monty Python's Flying Circus* TV shows, that the movie would be re-released to a much more receptive audience.

Victor Lownes, head of Playboy *in London, called me and said, "Would you like to come and have lunch?" And at lunch, he said, "I've just been watching* Python" – *these were the first episodes –* "I think it's the funniest thing I've seen on television for years, but American television is much too conservative to put this stuff out. But there are two thousand college cinemas and this stuff will be wonderful for American college students, so let's make a movie." Victor put half the money up and he found someone else to put up the other half. (John Cleese)*

I had to ask permission from the BBC to be allowed to take eight weeks off, unpaid leave, to do it. The BBC was happy to do that and that was quite nice. I was lucky. (Ian MacNaughton)

And Now for Something Completely Different begins with a short public service film, number forty-two in the series to be exact, which focuses on showing the viewer 'how not to be seen'. While the viewer is pondering just what it is that he or she would have to do in order to 'not be seen', they are transported to an idyllic woodland setting where they are informed that forty-seven fellow members of the British public are supposedly applying their skills at not being seen. The first of these is a certain Mr E. R. Bradshaw, of Napier Court, Black Lion Road, SE14, who, perhaps not too surprisingly, cannot be seen. When the cleverly concealed, and totally unsuspecting, Mr Bradshaw is asked to reveal himself, he is shot dead by an off-camera sniper, which clearly demonstrates the value of 'not being seen'.

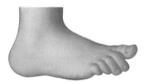

Trivia Fact: "And now for something completely different" is a phrase actually used during BBC broadcasts.

Mrs B. J. Smegma, of No. 13, The Crescent, Belmont, is also asked to emerge from her camouflage and suffers an equally horrible fate. A Mr Nesbitt, of Harlow, Newtown, no doubt after seeing what happened to Bradshaw and Smegma, proves somewhat reluctant to emerge from his hiding place. This slight inconvenience, however, is soon remedied when Nesbitt's cover is, quite literally, blown (to smithereens). A similar fate befalls Mr E. W. Lambert, of the Burrows, Oswestry, and also Mr and Mrs Watson of Hull, who had attempted to avoid death by incendiary device by going away on a two-week vacation, but were summarily dispatched after their whereabouts were given away by a bespectacled and knotted-hankie bedecked neighbour (Palin). The neighbour's treachery is repaid in triplicate when he is not only blown to smithereens, but his current dwelling and his birthplace are, as well.

The camera pans over to the chuckling narrator (Cleese), who is seated behind a desk in full evening dress (that's Cleese wearing the

dinner suit and not the desk), who introduces the movie by its title before being, you've guessed it, blown to smithereens.

It was extraordinary because the movie was a complete flop in America. Some idiot designed a poster with a happy snake with a funny hat on, and the adults looked at it and thought, 'kids' movie', and nobody went. In fact, I believe the movie took in less than they spent on the advertising – it was a total disaster. But it all went well in England where the sketches had already been transmitted, so it was all very scrambled! (John Cleese)

After a farcical Vaudevillian sketch featuring a man (Jones) whose sole means of entertaining his audience is by playing tunes like the French national anthem on a tape recorder lodged up one of his nostrils, the screen is suddenly filled by a sepia-toned photograph of the Houses of Parliament, while an accompanying voiceover announces that the then present-day British Empire (circa 1971) lay in ruins, and that London's streets were overrun with foreign nationals – mainly Hungarians. We are introduced to one of said Hungarian nationals (Cleese) who is standing at the counter within a traditional London tobacconist's attempting to purchase a packet of cigarettes by means of a recently-acquired Hungarian-English phrasebook. Imagine the poor shopkeeper's (Jones) consternation when the Hungarian standing before him states that "he will not buy this record, it is scratched."

"Ah, this is a tobacconists," the genial shopkeeper informs the Hungarian before pointing to the array of tobacco-related products adorning the shelves behind him, to which the Hungarian responds by saying that he won't be purchasing the tobacconists as it is scratched. No doubt encouraged by the fact that he has successfully managed to acquire a box of matches by informing the shopkeeper

Trivia Fact: During the making of *And Now for Something Completely Different*, Terry Gilliam asked esteemed animator Bob Godfrey whether he could borrow his camera. The answer was a prompt "bugger off," until Godfrey discovered that the younger animator was connected to Monty Python and lent his aid.

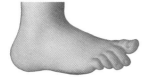

Trivia Fact: In 1988, Cleese received an Oscar nomination for *A Fish Called Wanda.*

Trivia Fact: Upon receiving his US draft notification, Gilliam enlisted in the National Guard and was stationed for basic training at Fort Dix, New Jersey. Whilst there, the aspiring animator was able to put his creative talent to good use by drawing flattering caricatures of his superiors in order to avoid the more mundane and unpleasant details of a lowly army private's life.

that his "hovercraft is full of eels", he consults the phrasebook again but further exasperates the shopkeeper by asking him if he wants to "come back to my place for 'bouncy bouncy'" and that he is "no longer infected". The indignant shopkeeper grabs the phrasebook from the Hungarian's hands and, in an attempt to rectify the situation, he selects what he believes to be a choice phrase but receives a punch in the face for his troubles. A bicycle-stealing police constable (Chapman) arrives at the scene only to be informed by the Hungarian that he has "beautiful thighs" and then be requested to "drop his panties, Sir Arthur", as the foreigner in his midst "cannot wait until lunchtime".

Fortunately for the Hungarian, who might otherwise have faced a lengthy stretch in prison, the originator of the wickedly deceptive phrasings (Palin) is brought to book (pun most certainly intended) and stands before a bewigged judge (Jones). The prosecuting council (Idle) provides damning guilt by reading out the phrase "could you please direct me to the nearest train station". which apparently translates into Hungarian as "please can you fondle my buttocks".

There was actually an instance where I can remember learning something – and that was when we had the 'Dirty Fork' sketch, the waiter comes in and commits suicide and everything. We'd done it on TV and it had been really funny, and we redid it – same sketch, same actors – and we showed it at an Odeon somewhere, and nobody laughed. I thought it was really weird, we'd seen people laugh before and it didn't get a titter, and the only thing I could see was that Ian had put a muzak track over it, sort of posh restaurant muzak, and I thought maybe that's just filling in all the gaps and just obliterating the film. We took the muzak off and then, when we showed it, people laughed at the sketch again. (Terry Jones)

CHAPTER THREE

Afterward comes another of Gilliam's animation scenes depicting rolling hills, which look remarkably like nipple-less breasts, sprouting trees in the shape of forearms with their branches (fingers) stretching up towards the sky, where more hands, representing birds, glide graciously across the screen. This is soon followed by my particular favourite animation from this Python movie, which shows an elderly gentleman humming a tune as he applies shaving foam to his throat and lower face. Rather than stop there, however, the old guy then continues applying more and more of the foam until his entire head is covered before picking up the cutthroat razor and lopping off his own head.

Trivia Fact: Whilst in high school, Gilliam was voted the 'pupil most likely to succeed' by his fellow students.

The next sketch features the decidedly dreary Arthur Pewtry (Palin) who, after becoming suspicious of his busty blonde bombshell of a wife, Deirdre (played by Carol Cleveland), decides to seek professional help in the form of a marriage guidance counselor (Idle). The cuckolded Pewtry's attempt to rescue his marriage is somewhat undermined by the counselor's apparent lust for the amorous Deirdre who, it seems, seeks more in the way of pleasure than totting up the sixpenny pieces housed within the holiday money bottle. Within minutes she has disappeared behind a changing screen, which for convenience's sake is situated near the far wall, to slip out of her comfortables and await the arrival of the by-now totally besotted counselor, who has politely asked Arthur to step outside into the gaudy anteroom for twenty minutes. It is against a backdrop of deific thunder and lightning, not to mention the muffled squealing and giggling coming from the office, that Arthur hears the voice of God, who berates him for his cowardly actions and orders him to go back in there, to fight like a man and to pull his finger out. Arthur, invigorated by God's holy rollicking, bounds into the counsellor's office and orders his wife to desist from

Trivia Fact: The only character to appear in all three Monty Python feature films is God.

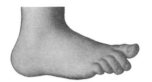

Trivia Fact: Mary Whitehouse would return to haunt one of the Pythons in 1977 when she brought a private prosecution for blasphemous libel against _Gay News_, the UK's first national gay liberation paper, which Graham Chapman had co-founded and lent financial support to. The editor of the newspaper, Denis Lemon, narrowly avoided nine months in jail for the publication of 'The Love That Dares to Speak its Name' – a poem by James Kirkup, a fellow of the Royal Society of Literature! (Whitehouse would also go on to be heavily involved in the campaign against _Life of Brian_.)

her infidelities and emerge from her love nest, only to be told in no uncertain terms to "go away". And 'go away' he does, rather timidly it has to be said, and it is here that Arthur learns an all-important lesson in that the 'meek' do not inherit the Earth after all; they have a sixteen-ton weight dropped upon them.

Arthur's squishing is soon forgotten, however, as the viewer is treated to another of Gilliam's bizarre animation montages featuring, amongst other things, a carnivorous man-eating pram which, after snaffling up several unsuspecting bystanders, hears another deific voice (this one feminine) and turns upon its handler; and an elasticized arm which, after several failed attempts, finally manages to snatch away the fig leaf covering Michelangelo's statue of David's naughty bits only to reveal the head of a woman looking suspiciously like Mary Whitehouse, the British suburban housewife and self-appointed 'Clean Up TV' campaigner.

Next up on screen is the hilariously funny 'Nudge Nudge, Wink Wink' sketch, featuring Idle portraying a spiv-like second-hand car salesman type, who foists himself upon a poor, unsuspecting upper-class businessman (Jones), in the lounge of a typical British pub. "Evening, squire," offers Idle's character, who, upon learning that his new-found best friend is married and from Purley, lures him into a 'mano-a-mano' conversation during which he hopes to elicit revealing personal information about the bewildered man's wife's sexual preferences. "Does she like photography?" he asks knowingly. "Nudge nudge, wink wink. Say no more."

"Do you mean holiday snaps?" asks the businessman innocently.

"Could be taken whilst on holiday, yes, could be," replies Idle's character earnestly, whilst looking as though he's imagining Mr and

Mrs Businessman holed up in some seedy hotel in Clacton-on-Sea engaging in sordid sex games possibly involving a bowler hat and umbrella, but then again a 'nod' is as good as a 'wink' to a blind bat. The piqued businessman finally tires of having a total stranger delving into his private life, and at last enquires as to what it is that the other is implying. It is only then that we discover that Mr 'Nudge Nudge' isn't quite the man-of-the-world he'd like us to believe him to be and hasn't actually been with a woman in the Biblical sense. The sketch ends with Gilliam dressed in nun's attire whilst miming to an overdubbed female voice denouncing sex as "overrated".

In the next sketch, a maniacal drill sergeant (Cleese), complete with three stripes sewn upon the sleeve of his decidedly dodgy looking PE kit, takes his totally disinterested recruits through the valuable lesson of how to disarm an assailant brandishing a banana. The reason for the recruits' total lack of interest is due to the fact that they have already learnt how to disarm would-be assailants brandishing apples, oranges, cherries (both red and black varieties), grapefruits (whole and segments), passion fruit and even mangos in syrup (nasty!). The drill sergeant, after calling upon Mr Apricot (a.k.a. Private Harrison) (Chapman), to attack him with a particularly nasty-looking banana, reveals to the other recruits that the best way to tackle a banana-wielding assailant is to shoot the man dead with a revolver before then disarming him by eating the aforementioned banana.

Trivia Fact: Idle's 'Nudge Nudge' character was chosen by Rowntrees for a series of TV commercials to promote the company's new 'Breakaway' biscuits.

Staying on a military theme, a British Army major (with an upper lip as stiff as the baton under his arm) apologizes to the audience for the silliness contained within the film before insisting that the director refrains from any more nonsense.

At first, the director appears to be in accordance with the major's wishes, as the following sketch is about a city living beneath a pall of fear as a result of a gang of 'Hell's Grannies' who roam the streets (streets where the surgical stocking is king) attacking defenceless young men. Apparently pension day is particularly hazardous, confesses a member of the local constabulary (Chapman) whilst standing in front of a wooden fence bearing the slogan 'make tea not love'.

Equally threatening are the dreaded 'Babysnatchers', a gang of adult-sized, diaper-wearing babies who pounce on unsuspecting mothers and steal their husbands. It is only when the director strays from the major's manifesto by featuring a vicious gang of 'left turn' signs that the major is compelled to make an official complaint. He then

Trivia Fact: Graham Chapman and his partner David Sherlock adopted a teenage runaway named John Tomiczek in 1971. Tomiczek, who had run away to London from his home in Liverpool, was treated for a fever by Chapman after approaching him on the street. After Chapman sent the boy home, he ran away again and returned to London. It was finally agreed that Chapman and Sherlock could adopt him, and Tomiczek eventually became Chapman's manager.

orders that the director show something decent and military, such as 'Precision Drilling', but is left feeling quite perturbed after witnessing a platoon of soldiers performing a highly-camp drill routine that wouldn't have been out of place in one of famous drag performer Danny La Rue's shows.

Afterward comes a brief Gilliam animation which, looking at it some twenty-five years later, could be construed as an early public information film warning about the dangers of excessive sunbathing, as it features an enchanted young prince that apparently ruled the 'land beyond the wobbles', who discovers a spot (melanoma) and dies three years later of cancer.

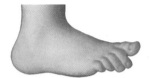

Trivia Fact: Idle's favourite football team is Sunderland A.F.C.

Next up is one of the highlights of the movie: the classic 'Expedition Interview' sketch which features an expedition leader (Cleese), who it seems suffers from double vision, interviewing a prospective candidate called Arthur Wilson, or Arthur Wilson(s) I & II depending on the expedition leader's point of view (both are played by Idle anyway). The expedition, which was initially designed to conquer both peaks of Kilimanjaro, hits an immediate snag when Wilson I, a fully qualified mountaineer as proscribed in the dictionary, points out that there is in fact only one Kilimanjaro, which would explain why the leader's brother failed to return from an earlier expedition designed to build a bridge between the two peaks. Upon enquiring as to how the expedition party will get to the mountain, he is informed that upon leaving Dover(s) they will head Africa(s)-ish to Nairobi(s), take the south road(s) for twelve miles and then ask.

"Does anyone speak Swahili?" enquires Arthur I.

"Oh yes, I think most of them do down there," replies the expedition leader.

Arthur(s) I & II are then introduced to Jimmy Blenkinsopp(s) I & II (Chapman), and although Arthur I is initially reassured by the Blenkinsopp(s) who are both thankfully aware of their leader's visual deficiencies, he flees into the hills (any except Kilimanjaro) after witnessing Blenkinsopp (not sure whether it's Blenkinsopp I or II) simulating the expedition's proposed route up the mountain by scrambling about the room and totally trashing the furniture whilst providing a running commentary. Arthur II, however, likes the idea and remains on board.

And then it's something for the men as the screen is filled with a close-up of a pair of bikini-clad breasts, followed by what appears to be some sort of outdoor Miss World contest with several other bikini-clad young ladies striking sultry poses for the cameraman who, judging from the lecherous off-screen noises, is clearly enjoying himself – until he zooms in upon a bikini-clad Cleese, and we're all very grateful that it's time for something completely different.

I was fully expecting Chapman's major to make an appearance at the end of this sketch, which is just downright silly. It features a flasher (Palin), complete with obligatory dirty raincoat, seen making his way along the street supposedly exposing himself to the female passers-by. Upon closer inspection, however, our would-be exhibitionist is found to be fully dressed beneath the shabby raincoat and has a sign with 'Boo' dangling around his midriff. Perhaps the major was waiting in the wings but was beaten to the draw by another of Gilliam's left-of-centre animations, with 'left' being the optimum word, as an unsuspecting Miss Spume is merrily tapping away at her typewriter when she falls victim to the dreaded International Communist Conspiracy, an army of fanatical fiends under the leadership of Mao Tse Tung. As the movie was made at the height of the Vietnam War, and given Gilliam's nationality, it isn't stretching the imagination too far to look upon the doomed Miss Spume, who is drowned in a sea of tiny yellow Maoists, as South Korea, and the galleon with sails bearing the stars and strips as the United States Army, which is clearly intent on saving other Miss Spumes, such as South Vietnam, from suffering a similar fate. This is closely followed by good ol' Uncle Sam himself who, using a rotting tooth as an analogy to show how Communism can undermine an unsuspecting democracy, informs us why nine out of ten small countries choose 'American Defence' or – to give it its proper title – Krelm toothpaste.

Trivia Fact: Terry Jones has been regularly writing columns in the English press that are highly critical of George Bush and Tony Blair's military policy since 9/11.

But enough of the Communist-threat analogies, and over to the Peephole Club, where a decidedly slimy-looking compere (Idle) is waiting to introduce Jones A. Newing (Jones) and his Musical Mice to a somewhat less-than-interested clientele. There are, Newing informs his audience, twenty-three white mice strategically placed within the elongated box standing on the stage in front of him, and each rodent lurking within has been painstakingly trained to squeak at any given pitch. The first tune in the mice's repertoire is, perhaps not surprisingly given that the mice are hidden within the box, 'Three Blind Mice', and our audience, although still seemingly disinterested, no doubt expects Newing to begin tugging on the mice's tails to elicit the tune. But oh no, nothing so mundane for the Peephole Club – Newing produces a pair of large mallets and, whilst humming the tune himself, begins pounding the mice to pulp, which certainly catches the audience's attention, not to mention their drinks, clothing, hair, etc.

We stay within the world of entertainment with 'It's the Arts', where the show's host 'Tom' (Cleese) is about to interview the renowned movie director Sir Edward Ross (Chapman). But before discussing the director's new movie he first attempts to bring a little informality to the proceedings by calling his guest 'Edward'. This, it seems, is okay by the director, as is 'Ted', which is apparently the diminutive that his close friends use, but the director draws the line at 'Eddie Baby' (well, he is a knight of the realm) and is equally offended by 'Sweetie', 'Sugarplum', 'Pussycat' and 'Angeldrawers'.

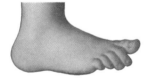

Trivia Fact: All four Beatles were fans of Monty Python.

"Well, how about 'Frank'?" enquires the host, before going on to explain that this was the name President Nixon apparently gave to his pet hedgehog.

Sir Edward is most certainly not amused and starts to walk off set, but is lured back to his seat when the genial host not only refers to him by his correct name, but also asks the director to talk about his latest movie. Sir Edward begins by taking the audience back to the halcyon days of 1919, when he was but a humble Hollywood tea boy, but by now Tom has lost interest and brings a halt to the proceedings. Tom's timing couldn't have been more perfect (at least from a male perspective) as a seductive temptress (Cleveland) wearing a revealing black negligee lures an unsuspecting, and by now thoroughly-aroused, milkman (Palin) into the house, up the stairs and into her bedroom, where he is incarcerated alongside two dozen other forlorn milkmen.

Whether the milkmen will ever escape is of no concern to us now, and we bid them a fond farewell as we arrive upon Ernest Scribbler, who is

about to think up a joke so lethal that anyone reading it will also die – including himself, and his mother, who'd unfortunately assumed that the joke was her son's suicide note.

The joke, which was found to be devastating up to a range of fifty yards, was 80,000 times more powerful than the 'Trebor' joke used at Munich. In fact, it was considered so deadly that the British Army's top brass decided to have the joke translated into the German language so that it could be unleashed upon the Bosch during the Ardennes Offensive of 18 July 1944. German casualties were appalling and played a vital part in bringing about an end to the war in Europe.

Trivia Fact: Michael Palin's father suffered from a serious stutter, which no doubt proved a great help for the role of stuttering, animal-loving jewel thief Ken Pile in *A Fish Called Wanda*, for which he won a BAFTA for Best Supporting Actor.

H. M. GOVERNMENT WARNING: Here is the world's funniest joke, translated back into English where possible, which, although less potent than the fully translated German version, can still be lethal. Read on at your peril.

"If that is git only Stucco and Slotermeyer?"

"Yes!"

"Celebration dog that, or the Flipperwaldt Gersput!"

Before we continue I'd like to take time out to offer my condolences to the families for those of you that didn't heed the warning...

After another brief Gilliam-esque interlude involving, amongst other things, an apology from Richard III for the previous scene's bad taste, we are transported to a city which has become so overcrowded that motor cars have taken the law into their own hands (or should that be steering wheels?). Time, however, (not to mention gas) is running out for these so-called 'killer cars' because, thanks to the wonders of atomic mutation, there's a new sheriff in town in the form of a giant Siamese cat, which stalks the capital in search of the motorized menaces.

But the monstrous moggy must not be content with chewing on cars, and just when it seems that the city will be eaten, the Earth trembles, and the Sun is blotted from the sky – presumably by the swarms of giant bees which fill the air – and 300,000,000 armoured horsemen covered with coats of a thousand different colours appear at every street corner attacking the monster cat in a scene of such spectacular proportions that it could never in your life be seen (in live action) in a low budget movie such as this. Just as the monster cat is weakening, the Earth splits apart with a deafening roar... and tumbles into a mincer (as in grinding machine and not a soldier from the camp platoon seen in an earlier sketch), but all is apparently well. And how do we know this? Because we are treated to a brief musical interlude whilst gazing upon a naked water nymph – that's how, silly!

And now for something completely unforgettable: the classic 'Parrot' sketch featuring a pet-store owner (Palin), a disgruntled customer (Cleese) and a dead parrot (a Norwegian Blue called Polly).

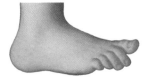

Trivia Fact: The 'Parrot' sketch is based on an improv theatre game in which two participants compete during a scene to see whether they can make the other person repeat themselves.

The reason behind the customer's disgruntlement is that the aforementioned parrot he purchased from the pet shop earlier in the day appears to be "dead", "demised", "passed on", "ceased to be", "expired", "gone to its maker" and, my own particular favourite, "run down the curtain and joined the choir." The store's owner refuses to accept this and suggests that the parrot, which at this point is lying on the bottom of the cage, is merely "resting", and after the irate customer disproves this theory by bashing the parrot several times against the counter he claims that the bird has now been "stunned" just as it was waking up. The Northern Blue apparently stuns easily. (In a continuity error, Cleese's arms alternate between being crossed and placed on his hips throughout the sketch.) The customer then tries a different tack by enquiring as to why the parrot had been nailed to its perch, but the storekeeper is ready and blithely informs the customer that Norwegian Blues pine for their native fjords and the nailing of the bird's feet to the perch was simply a preventative measure to stop it from escaping.

The storekeeper finally decides to adhere to the old adage that 'the customer is always right', but confesses that he cannot replace the bird as he's "out of parrots" and offers a compromise by way of a "slug".

CHAPTER THREE

"Does it talk?" enquires the customer, but the pet shop owner is past caring about slugs, customers, parrots, the store and his life in general, for he has a burning ambition to be a cross-dressing lumberjack...

Once again, it's time for something completely different – and to emphasize this point we are treated to a brief scene where Cleese is being spit-roasted, before we arrive at the next sketch, acted out within a seemingly high-class London restaurant where a diner (Chapman) has been given grubby cutlery in the form of a 'dirty fork'. The waiter (Jones) is most apologetic, as is the head waiter (Palin) who threatens to sack the entire kitchen staff, and also the restaurant's manager (Idle), but the head chef, the temperamental Mongo (Cleese) takes exception to the complaint and threatens all and sundry with a meat cleaver. This is clearly all too much for the manager, who commits hari-kari with the dirty fork (and heaven only knows what might have happened had the diner informed the waiter about the dirty knife).

Trivia Fact: The 'Parrot' sketch was selected as the number one alternative comedy sketch of all time by a Radio Times poll in 2004. It received twice as many votes as the number two sketch, the 'Four Yorkshiremen' sketch, also by Python. Monty Python also appeared at number six on the list, with 'Ministry of Silly Walks', and number ten, with 'The Spam Song'.

I do remember an extraordinary experience: The first time we showed And Now for Something Completely Different, *there was hilarious laughter up to fifty minutes, then the audience went very quiet for twenty, twenty-five minutes, and then they came up again and finished very well. So we took all that middle material, put it at the beginning, and it all worked beautifully up to about fifty minutes, and then the audience got quiet! We discovered that whatever order we put the material in, at about fifty minutes they stopped laughing. And in order to get people to go with you past the fifty-minute mark, they have to know what's going to happen next. In other words, you have to have characters that they care about and a story they can enjoy and believe in. There's a huge learning curve.*
(John Cleese)

After a brief musical interlude, presumably to clear away the disused and decidedly dirty cutlery, not to mention the dead bodies, we swiftly move along to witness a robbery in progress. Unfortunately for the bank robber (Cleese), the bank that he is attempting to rob contains neither large quantities of money or easily transportable bags of cash, and is left somewhat bemused when the attendant (Idle) informs him that the bank is actually a lingerie store. Not to be outdone, the robber absconds with a pair of women's panties (perhaps he's also a closet lumberjack).

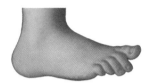

Trivia Fact: Terry Gilliam was *Harry Potter* author J. K. Rowling's first choice to direct the films of her novels. However, Warner Brothers instead selected *Home Alone* director Chris Columbus for the job.

Next up is the 'Falling Past the Window' sketch which features two business employees (Cleese and Idle) merrily engaged in what it is that they're doing, when one happens to glance towards the window and sees a work colleague plummeting to his death. It is only upon witnessing a further two suicides – one of which is definitely Wilkins from finance, and another of which may have been Robertson – sailing past their office window that the pair realise there must be a board meeting in progress. They then place a £5 wager on whether poor old "Parkinson" will make it a "hat-trick".

After this comes another mind-boggling Gilliam animation featuring a ten-legged humanoid creature which is seen clambering into bed before then emerging the following morning from beneath the quilt as a bizarre man-butterfly hybrid.

In the next sketch, Herbert Anchovy (Palin), in the all-too-familiar shoes of those who realize that they are in the wrong profession, is bored with his lot as an accountant and seeks the services of a Vocational Guidance Counsellor (Cleese), who, after conducting several lengthy interviews and aptitude tests that indicate that his client is appallingly dull, drab and has no sense of humour, arrives at the conclusion that Herbert's future lies in, you've guessed it, accountancy.

But then Herbert, who has spent the last twenty years as an accountant, confesses that he wants to be a lion-tamer and wants to start in his new role at 9am the following morning because he has a lion-tamer's hat which apparently lights up in the dark but, not only that, it is tax-deductible under paragraph 335. The counsellor tries to dissuade Herbert, as this is quite a radical change, and therefore suggests that it might be best if Herbert made the transition into lion-taming via banking or insurance. Herbert, however, remains steadfast in his desire to be a lion-tamer, and although he has no experience in lion taming, this should present no problem for him, as he has seen them in the zoo – they are small brown furry creatures with stubby little legs.

It is only upon learning that the creature he is describing is actually an anteater, and being shown a terrifying close-up of a charging lion, that Herbert elects for an alternative career in the world of banking, for it is a man's life, filled with thrills and romance, and he admits that he only wanted to be a lion-tamer so that he might live to see his name in lights. And so he does, thanks to his fairy Godmother (Idle).

And now it's over to the TV studios and the show that no one wants to appear on – *Blackmail*. After a brief introduction from the slimy host (Palin), complete with tiger-skin jacket, slicked-back hair and a removable moustache, it's straight up to Preston, Lancashire, where an unsuspecting Mrs Betty Teal is forced into paying £15 to stop the show from revealing the name of her lover in Bolton. As the adulterous Mrs Teal is calling in with her 'donation', we are treated to a brief musical interlude by the show's buck-naked pianist (Jones) – buck-naked, that is, except for the white collar and Dickie bowtie that he's wearing. Next up is Mr 'S' of Bromsgrove, an MP and a Mason who, unless willing to meet the show's demands, will have not only his name exposed on air, but also those of the three other people involved, the youth organization for which they worked, and the store where he bought the equipment (and I don't think we're talking Wal-Mart here, folks).

Trivia Fact: Because of the limited budget for the film, the Pythons had to forego the luxury of a soundstage; hence the team's decision to film in an abandoned dairy.

Our next unsuspecting victim, I mean contestant, is seen making his way down a respectable-looking suburban street and into a house where a dominatrix is waiting to flagellate him for an undisclosed fee, but whatever the woman is charging per stroke is peanuts compared

Trivia Fact: An oil painting by Heidi Harrington of Terry Jones sitting at a piano naked toured the United Kingdom in 2004.

to the 'guilt-o-meter' at the right-hand corner of the screen, which is adding increments of £300 for every few minutes the blackmailee remains in a compromising position, accompanied by the ker-ching of a cash register opening (music to the host's ears). A grand total of £3,000 is amassed before the contestant finally contacts the studio and concedes defeat. As the by now decidedly-richer host conducts his latest transaction over what I'm presuming to be a gold-coloured telephone, but which could well be made of eighteen-carat gold with all the sordid cash flowing in, the show's address where all moneys are to be deposited appears on screen:

Blackmail
Behind the hot-water pipes,
Third washroom along,
Victoria Station,
London.

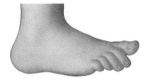

Trivia Fact: John Cleese was voted the second greatest comedian of all time on the show *The Comedian's Comedian*, which aired on the UK's Channel 4 on 1 January 2005. Eric Idle came in at twenty-one, and Michael Palin at thirty.

Cut to the major, who is clearly caught off-guard by the unexpected intrusion and quickly, rather too quickly for my liking, terminates his telephone conversation. Was it he who was caught on camera and will be shortly hailing a cab to Victoria Station to deposit £3,000 behind the aforementioned hot-water pipes? No matter, for we must depart for Sheffield, Yorkshire, as we have been invited to a local playing field to watch the town's women's group performing their annual historical re-enactment. The group's spokeswoman (Idle), who is dressed in twin-set and pearls, and clutching a rather nice handbag, informs the interviewer that she and her colleagues are extremely interested in modern works, and were the first group to perform *Camp on Blood Island*, not to mention the extremely popular re-enactment of Nazi war atrocities. This year's re-enactment, we are informed, will be the Battle of Pearl Harbor. But how, we wonder, can this small clique of civil-minded housewives perform such a massive re-enactment – for the playing field is absent of vital props such as US Navy uniforms, a battleship such as the USS Arizona or even a Japanese Zero fighter plane. Such minor details are soon rendered inconsequential, however, as the housewives reveal the true horrors of that fateful Sunday of 8 December 1941 by engaging in a bout of mud-wrestling.

Next is a musical interlude featuring a young couple, Brian and Elspeth, locked in a passionate embrace as sexual imagery – such as a train entering a tunnel, a Scotsman tossing a caber, a cockerel and a tower being demolished (but shown in reverse) – flash across the screen. Unfortunately for poor, frustrated Elspeth, these are not sublimated sexual allegories at all, but rather snippets of films from her not-so-amorous lover's private collection.

And so without further ado we come to the final sketch of the movie, featuring the annual 'upper-class twit' competition which is being staged at Brambly Park. The running commentary is provided by an off-camera Cleese, who before introducing the contestants informs us that the "going is firm under foot", and that there's "no sign of rain".

The five contestants are as follows:
1. Vivian Smith-Smyth-Smith (Cleese), who is a member of the Grenadier Guards, and can count to four.
2. Simon Zinc-Trumpet Harris (Idle), an Old Etonian, and married to a very attractive table lamp.
3. Nigel Incubator-Jones (Jones), whose best friend is a tree, and who is a stockbroker in his spare time (presumably that's Jones and not the tree).
4. Gervais Brook-Hamster (Palin), who's in the wine trade, except, that is, when his father is using him as a wastepaper basket.
5. Oliver St John-Mollusk (Chapman), another Old Etonian, whose father is a cabinet minister and whose mother won the Derby, and who is thought by many to be this year's outstanding twit.

The first event of the afternoon is the 'Walking in a Straight Line', which, apparently, is Oliver's worst event. They're under starter's orders and they're off, or not as it turns out, but eventually the dim-witted inbreds toddle off towards the second event: the Matchbox Jump, which will see the contestants having to successfully leap over two layers of matchboxes, and will surely give us an insight as to the early favourites. As suspected, the double layer of boxes proves too

Trivia Fact: A new species of lemur discovered in Madagascar has been named after John Cleese, in recognition of his work calling the plight of lemurs to attention. Its scientific name is Avahi cleesei.

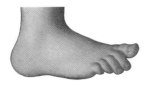

Trivia Fact: An asteroid, originally classified Asteroid 13681 and discovered by a pair of Czech astronomers, was officially named 'Monty Python' in 1997. In addition, six asteroids discovered by a team of Swedish astronomers working in Chile between 1992 and '93 were named after each of the individual Pythons.

much for Oliver who falls, and also for Vivian, who refuses. The next event is 'Shooting the Rabbit', and the organizers have attempted to make things easy for the contestants by staking each rabbit to the ground so as to make an easier target, but unfortunately even this task proves too much for Oliver, who somehow manages to run himself over with his own sports car.

The fourth event in this riveting contest is perhaps the most difficult for our contestants, as they will have to remove a bra from a debutante, but as these clods are never likely to get their hands on real women the organizers have been forced to use mannequins. Simon is obviously an old hand at removing his spousal table lamp, for he emerges as the leader, closely followed in second place by Nigel, who has no doubt been spurred on by his leafy chum, who can be seen in the distance.

And now for the fifth and final event, which is always a crowd-pleaser, as the first contestant who manages to shoot himself will be declared this year's winner. But even this seemingly straightforward act is beyond Nigel, who misses from point-blank range, as does Simon, although by way of a consolation he does manage to shoot Vivian. Gervais, the part-time wastepaper basket from Kensington, however, has no such problems and is declared the (albeit posthumous) winner. Second place goes to Vivian of Mayfair by default, and third place is awarded to Simon, also of Kensington.

CHAPTER FOUR: MONTY PYTHON AND THE HOLY GRAIL

We're Knights of the Round Table
We dance when e'er we're able,
We do routines and chorus scenes
With footwork impecc-able
We dine well here in Camelot
We eat ham and jam and spam a lot...

In 1974 Messrs Chapman, Idle, Gilliam, Jones and Palin were reunited with their former Python comrade-in-comedy, John Cleese, who had left after the third *Flying Circus* series, to once again bring their unique brand of eclectic humour to the big screen. This time, however, rather than attempt to emulate their earlier success with *And Now for Something Completely Different*, the team decided against making another compilation movie, and instead elected to use for subject matter that most quintessential of English legends: King Arthur and the Knights of the Round Table.

The filming, which cost an estimated £230,000, was completed sometime in 1974, and the finished movie was first premiered in Los Angeles, California, in March 1975 and again in London the following month; before the London premiere, in typical Python fashion an advert was placed stating that the first 10,000 punters through the door would receive a free coconut!

Python always had a strong desire to work on movies, so when the TV series finished it wasn't hard to talk us into doing one. (Michael Palin)

Sometimes I enjoyed performing more. In film, I loved the scene in Grail *where the guard is told not to leave the room till anyone, etc., because the first time it went right and it's there on film. It just felt funny – all one*

Trivia Fact: *Monty Python and the Holy Grail* was voted the fifth greatest comedy film of all time by *Total Film* magazine in 2000.

take. Well done, Jonesy. I have to say I love filming for Jonesy. (Eric Idle) The glossy colour pamphlet accompanying the 'Special Edition' DVD of *Monty Python and the Holy Grail*, which was released in 2004 (see Appendix Two for more catalogue information), claims to have been some twenty-six years in the making, and involved much trawling through the Python vaults to unearth materials which had, up until this time, believed to have been lost to history and were almost as elusive as the fabled Grail itself. The bulk of Python's archive is listed in a huge tome nicknamed, somewhat ironically, 'The Bible' – which, if printed out, would give the original good book a run for its money size-wise – so you can easily understand that finding everything at the drop of a hat is hardly an easy task, and thus some projects take longer than others.

There was quite a lot of debate about [who should play Arthur]. I think in the end nobody wanted to do it. (Terry Jones)

No one wanted to sacrifice the chance of playing lots of silly smaller roles in order to play the one big one. (Michael Palin)

Seems obvious now, doesn't it? I think I was quite keen for Graham to do it. I'm not sure, I can't even remember whether I thought Graham would be a great idea, or whether I was in favour of Eric doing it. (Terry Jones)

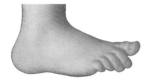

Trivia Fact: A significant part of the movie's funding was provided by Led Zeppelin, Genesis and Pink Floyd, with the latter group donating royalties from their *Dark Side of the Moon* album. The members of Floyd were apparently such avid fans of the *Monty Python's Flying Circus* TV show that they would even interrupt recording in order to watch it.

Disc one of the two-disc 'Special Edition' DVD boasts such previously unobtainable bounty as a 'high definition wide-screen presentation' (with pink frilly edges), enlightening commentaries by directors Terry Gilliam and Terry Jones, plus general complaints and back biting by the rest of the team and an exciting 'Follow the Killer Rabbit' feature. Perhaps most wondrous of all, however, are the twenty-four seconds – yes, twenty-four seconds – of hitherto previously unseen footage (reported to have been removed just before the movie's original release). Though an additional twenty-four seconds may not seem like much to the casual observer, to dedicated Python aficionados the inclusion of the deleted scene will seem like gazing upon the Holy Grail itself.

It is perhaps worth mentioning that the decision (quest?) to include this additional footage caused the production team the greatest of difficulties. Although the team had kept hold of the original negative of the deleted scene, the sound elements were of such poor quality that their re-introduction threatened to ruin the movie's timing. Thanks to modern digital technology, however, the problem was resolved.

Pink Floyd put in some money – not a huge amount, but they earn from it to this day. That's why they're rich. Without Python they'd be nowhere! (Michael Palin)

Disc two contains special features, such as an opportunity for all you budding Python-spians to participate in a mindless sing-along on three of the movie's songs, plus the chance to join Michael Palin and Terry Jones on their special quest in returning to the *Holy Grail* locations such as Castle Stalker, the Sixteenth Century castle situated some twenty-five miles north of Oban on Scotland's west coast, Glen Coe and Doune Castle, the Fourteenth Century castle in Perthshire, which was where most of the filming actually took place. Doune Castle has come to be looked upon as something of a shrine for visiting Python fans, who can even avail themselves of a specially-made set of coconut hooves and merrily canter about the castle grounds whilst shouting out lines from the script.

Setting up Holy Grail *was just so problematic. We had five weeks to shoot it in. Terry and I had been all over Scotland and then all over Wales looking for locations, and we decided on Scotland. We'd picked all these wonderful castles, and then two weeks before we were due to start filming we suddenly got this letter from the Department of the Environment of Scotland saying we couldn't use any of their castles. I was in panic. Terry and I'd been planning to go up and go through everything and make sure we knew exactly where our cameras were going to be, and instead of doing that, we found ourselves rushing around trying to find new locations for the whole film. It was a nightmare. We ended up with Doune Castle – that had to be three castles – and then we came up with Castle Stalker for the ending.* (Terry Jones)

Special Edition DVD

Among the many home-video releases of *Monty Python and the Holy Grail*, the DVD 'Special Edition' is most recommended for its exhaustive list of special features, including two commentary tracks, documentaries related to the film, the 'Camelot Song' as sung by Lego men and 'Subtitles for People Who Don't Like the Film', consisting of lines taken from Shakespeare's *Henry IV, Part II*, specially selected to match the film's dialogue. There are also two scenes synchronised in Japanese, where the knights search for a 'holy sake cup'.

The DVD 'Special Edition' includes 'The Quest for the Holy Grail Locations', which shows places in Scotland used for 'England 932 AD'. Many scenes were filmed in or around Doune Castle; 'Scene 24' and the bloodthirsty rabbit's 'Cave of Caerbannog' were in sight of Loch Tay, near Killin; and 'The Bridge of Death' was in Glen Coe. In the closing battle scene, shots facing 'Castle Aaaargh' were filmed at Castle Stalker but the shots looking the other way towards the huge army were filmed later somewhere near Stirling once they'd managed to get enough people.

– From Wikipedia.com

The disc also includes 'Monty Python and the Holy Grail in Lego', 'On Location With the Pythons' – an eighteen-minute on-location report by BBC's *Film Night* originally broadcast on 19 December 1974 – plus Terry Gilliam's original sketches, behind-the-scenes photographs, unused ideas, movie posters and theatrical trailers.

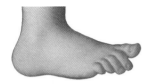

Trivia Fact: The alternate title of '*Dentist on the Job*' is 'Get On With It!'

Trivia Fact: Michael Palin plays ten roles in the film, the most overall.

Upon inserting disc one into your trusty DVD recorder, you sit back and await the movie – so imagine the surprise you'll have upon seeing the TV screen suddenly filled with grainy black and white images, and the opening credits from the decidedly dodgy movie 'Dentist on the Job', an early big-screen outing for TV comic Bob Monkhouse, who would later show up in the first *Carry On* movie *Sergeant* – only this first movie hardly had any of the *Carry On* team's classic pace for gags, and the movie's only redeeming feature is the inclusion of the delectable Shirley Eaton, who would go on to find lasting acclaim as the gold paint girl in the 1964 James Bond movie *Goldfinger*. For some inexplicable reason I must have been distracted from seeing Gilliam's opening animation sketch depicting the Holy Grail appearing through the clouds before shooting up into the stratosphere, and begun cursing my misfortune for having purchased a faulty DVD (well, these things do happen...), but just as I was reaching for the remote control the cheesy movie mercifully ground to a halt and the screen suddenly went blank for several seconds before finally introducing the title credit for the intended movie. It was only then that we realised that we had been duped, and I swore that I could almost hear Eric Idle cackling wildly in my head (and I suspect that I wasn't the only one... go on, admit it!).

People like Led Zeppelin put in ten grand. Tim Rice coughed up. But the reason there are coconut shells, and not horses, is because they couldn't afford horses! (Neil Innes)

CHAPTER FOUR

Next up are the opening credits, but even here the Pythons are unable to restrain themselves and the viewer is drawn to the pigeon-Swedish postscripts that appear at the bottom of each page offering subliminal suggestions that we might consider taking a holiday in Sweden to see the lovely lakes and the equally-wonderful telephone system, not forgetting the country's many wonderful animals, principally the majestic moose, which apparently once bit the subtitles editor's sister while she was carving her initials with the sharpened end of an interspace toothbrush. Whilst we, the viewers, or perhaps that should be 'readers', are pondering what it was that caused the naughty girl to carry out such an abhorrent attack on the moose, we are informed that the subtitles editor has been sacked for dereliction of duty, followed by subsequent announcements that his or her successors have also been shown the door for similar offences, which included an overkill on the word 'llama'.

Filming is an appallingly technical process, doing the same business over and over and over again from different angles, and on the whole directors forget – I'm not talking about our directors, because they're good on it – but most directors simply do not understand the process that actors need. And when I'm working, I will sometimes say, "All right, we've got the technical stuff settled, now it's the actors' turn. Let's do four or five takes back-to-back." Because what happens is you get warmed up. What normally happens is you do the first take and then it stops while somebody adjusts this bulb, this light, somebody adjusts the position of a lamp, somebody else comes and takes some fluff off your jacket, somebody else is worried about the fact that there's a bit of glow on your nose. By the time you're ready to shoot again, you're cold again. (John Cleese)

Trivia Fact: *Holy Grail* was Elvis Presley's favourite comedy film. Legend has it that the King owned a copy for every room in his Graceland mansion, and it wasn't out of the question for Elvis and his trusted 'Memphis Mafia' to watch the movie up to three times in one day!

At last the movie is about to begin, and we are taken back through the swirling mists of time to 932 AD, the period that historians refer to as the 'Dark Ages', the time of Arthur Pendragon, King of the Britons, his fabled Knights of the Round Table, and their quest to seek out the Holy Grail.

The sound of approaching horses fills the bleak rural landscape, but rather than find King Arthur (Chapman) appearing out of the mist mounted upon a magnificent charger befitting the King of the Britons, we see our hero jauntily skipping along on foot whilst mimicking the actions of someone on horseback, with his faithful manservant Patsy (Gilliam) following behind banging two empty coconut shells together to simulate the sound of beating hooves. (It is one thing to suspect that this was perhaps how the pioneer movie producers of the early westerns achieved this sound effect, but to see it so blatantly exposed was pure brilliance on the part of the Pythons.)

The intrepid duo arrive at a castle, where Arthur informs the sentry of their identities and that they have travelled the length and breadth of the land in search of knights who might join their court at Camelot, only to be subjected to a discussion on the migratory habits of swallows and the creature's supposed inability to single-wingedly transport a coconut.

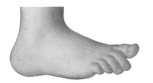

Trivia Fact: Gilliam suffers the most deaths during the movie, four in total: as the Green Knight, Bors, the Bridgekeeper and the Animator.

The movie then cuts away to an animated scene featuring a Terry Gilliam sequence of Brueghel prints, accompanied by incessant wailing, groaning and discordant medieval music. The last Brueghel image disappears from our screens to be replaced by a live action shot of a contorted upside-down face, no doubt contorted as a result of the leg that has just fallen across it. The camera then slowly pans away to reveal a rickety wooden cart, already straining under the weight of several dead corpses, being led through a plague-ridden village – with the black-hooded cartmaster (Idle) walking behind the cart chanting "bring out yer dead".

It is whilst the cartmaster is otherwise occupied in discussing the merits of accepting his usual fee of 9p for the body of one who has not quite succumbed to the disease that King Arthur and Patsy are seen making their way through the village.

"Who's that, then?" the not-quite-dead man's relative enquires of the cartmaster.

"I dunno," replies the cartmaster, "must be a king."

"Why?"

"He hasn't got shit all over him."

You don't direct comedy; you just avoid trying to get in the way of people being funny! You must understand that the rest of us have a healthy contempt for directors. This was the least-wanted job; obviously the two who wanted it got it. Since they are both control freaks (as are all directors), it drove them both mad. But Terry G. won; he drove Terry J. madder! Terry J. would be cutting by day; Terry G. would undo it and be re-cutting by night. In the end, the balance worked great. Terry J. is good with the acting, Terry G. is good with the location feel, the sinister boat, the visual elements. (Eric Idle)

Arthur and Patsy continue on their search and at last come upon a castle in the distance. When Arthur stops to enquire of a group of peasants working the surrounding fields as to which knight lives within, he is confronted by one of the peasants (Palin) who not only refuses to accept that the man standing before him is indeed his sovereign, but also informs Arthur that Britain is a dictatorship, and a self-perpetuating autocracy, which aims to keep the working classes firmly downtrodden. Arthur becomes exasperated and, as a means of showing the peasants that he is indeed their king, he explains how the Lady of the Lake emerged from the bosom of the water, her arm clad in the purest shimmering samite, and presented him with Excalibur to signify Divine Providence.

Palin's character 'Dennis', a Tenth Century Karl Marx, is unmoved by this and retorts by dismissing Arthur's claim because "strange women lying in ponds distributing swords is no basis for a system of government" and that "you can't expect to wield supreme executive power just 'cause some watery tart threw a sword at you!"

Arthur decides against becoming embroiled in an argument over the rights and wrongs of Tenth Century anarcho-syndicalism, and the rights of the common peasant, and continues on his quest to find like-minded men who will assist him in seeking the Grail. It is while he is going about his search that he and Patsy emerge from a forest and happen upon a clearing where two knights are locked in mortal combat. The larger of the two knights, dressed head to foot in black armour, and sounding remarkably like John Cleese, eventually slays his green-armoured opponent (an unseen Gilliam), and Arthur is so impressed by the Black Knight's fighting prowess that he invites the knight to join him at Camelot. But the Black Knight not only refuses to accept Arthur's offer, he also refuses to allow Arthur and Patsy to cross the wooden bridge that fords a nearby stream. Arthur, although anxious to be on his way, has little option but to accept the Black Knight's challenge.

Trivia Fact: Two nuns with huge mallets can be spotted at the beginning of the plague cart scene; they were originally meant to be hitting the man on the cart with them, but this scene was cut.

Trivia Fact: Anarcho-syndicalism is a form of anarchism in which labor unions are the focus of social change. Anarcho-syndicalists seek to end wage labor and private ownership, and replace capitalism and the state with a worker-run democracy for all. Many of the original American labor unions were anarcho-syndicalist.

Trivia Fact: Contrary to normal practice on a Monty Python set, all the female roles in the movie were played by actual women, with the exception of Dennis' mother, who was played by Terry Jones.

The Black Knight scene made me fall off my sofa laughing. "Your legs off"... yeah, right! (Neil Innes)

The ensuing fight, which is generally regarded as one of the most hilarious scenes in the entire movie, sees Arthur proving victorious, but only after hacking off the Black Knight's four limbs. The Black Knight, upon losing his left arm at the shoulder, refuses to yield and dismisses the wound as little more than a scratch. The fight resumes and Arthur, after hacking off the Black Knight's right arm, which is perhaps far more significant in that it was his opponent's sword arm, drops to his knees and begins offering thanks to the Lord for having granted him this victory, but the Black Knight has other ideas and runs at Arthur and kicks him in the head, and continues kicking his regal adversary in the hope of gaining a submission. Arthur then hacks off the Black Knight's legs, but even then his limbless adversary refuses to concede defeat and offers to settle for a draw.

It is there that we take a temporary leave of Arthur and Patsy and instead are transported to a tranquil village scene – tranquil except for the Latin chanting coming from a procession of monks (led by Neil Innes) who are making their way through the village stopping occasionally to smack themselves on the foreheads with the wooden boards they are each carrying.

As the monks continue with their chanting and self-flagellation they pass a group of villagers who are dragging a young woman dressed as a witch, complete with pointy hat and a turnip strapped to her face as a false nose, through the streets towards the ruins upon the hill overlooking the village. The villagers present the witch (played by John Cleese's then-wife Connie Booth) to Sir Bedevere the 'Wise' (Jones) and seek permission from the sagacious knight to burn the girl.

It is while Sir Bedevere is questioning the villagers' reasoning for having accused the girl of witchcraft that Arthur and Patsy hove into view and watch the ensuing discussions in which one villager (Cleese) informs Sir Bedevere that the girl must be a witch as she had turned him into a newt. When Sir Bedevere lapses into silence to ponder this allegation the villager reluctantly admits that he has since "got better".

Sir Bedevere informs the silenced crowd that there are indeed ways to determine whether the girl is a witch and enquires as to how they themselves would seek the proof. The unanimous response is for burning the girl at the stake and upon hearing this, the seemingly-not-so-sagacious Sir Bedevere, leads the dim-witted villagers into a farcical debate that results in the unfortunate girl being hauled away to the nearest stake on the evidence that a witch's weight was equal to that of a duck. The knight's foolproof logic apparently being that in order for a witch to burn she would have to be made of wood, and everyone is in agreement that both wood and ducks float upon the water (not to mention bread, apples, gravy and very small rocks).

Trivia Fact: When the villagers approach Sir Bedevere, the knight can be seen attempting to attach a coconut to a swallow, probably to test the theory from an earlier scene. This is subtle Python humour at its best.

Arthur is so impressed by the knight, who has indeed proved himself most wise in the ways of science, that he invites Sir Bedevere to accompany him to Camelot and be the first to join his number at the Round Table. They are soon joined on their journey by Sir Gawain (Gilliam), Sir Galahad the Pure (Palin), Sir Lancelot the Brave (Cleese) and last but not least Sir Robin (Idle), who was apparently not so brave as Sir Lancelot, who had nearly fought the Dragon of Angora, who had nearly stood up to the vicious Chicken of Bristol and who had personally wet himself at the Battle of Baden Hill, and the aptly named Sir Not Appearing in This Film.

Trivia Fact: During the witch scene Eric Idle starts to chuckle (and who can blame him?) and can be seen biting on his scythe in an attempt to stifle his mirth.

Trivia Fact: One of the villagers in the witch scene is actually ex-Beatle George Harrison.

Together they, their pages and Sir Robin's merry band of musicians (the lute-playing leader is played by Neil Innes, who wrote the songs featured in the movie) continue on their quest.

And so King Arthur leads his knights back to Camelot, only for Patsy to rain on the king's parade by revealing that the castle is nothing more than a cheap model. Their stay at the one-dimensional Camelot, however, is but a brief one for God (or Gilliam's seemingly pissed-off animated deity, which bears a striking resemblance to the Nineteenth Century cricketer W. G. Grace) appears in the sky and sets Arthur, King of the Britons, and his Knights of the Round Table, the task of searching for the Holy Grail.

They set forth across the land and eventually arrive upon a castle where Arthur, after informing one of the guards (Cleese) of his identity and how he has been charged by God with a sacred quest to seek the Grail, requests that he and his men be given food and shelter, and suggests that his master, a certain Guy de Loimbard, might like to join

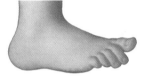

Trivia Fact: The other musicians belonging to Sir Robin's troupe were members of an English folk band called Saltwater Sealion.

their number. The guard replies (in heavily-accented pidgeon French) by informing the astounded knights that his master has no need to join them on their quest for he already has a nice grail, thank you very much. It is while Arthur is pondering this revelation that he discovers that the guards are French, and when they refuse to allow him to see the grail he threatens to storm the castle.

The French guard responds by threatening to fart in Arthur's general direction, before likening his mother to a hamster, and going on to declare that Arthur's father "smelt of elderberries". Whilst Arthur is demanding that the French give in to his demands the guard shouts the immortal line "Fetchez la vache!" ('Bring the cow!')

Arthur and his knights stand by helplessly as the cow comes hurtling over the battlements and lands upon Sir Galahad's page. Whether it was in response to the page's murder, or the fact that the poor unfortunate cow had died without having first been milked, Arthur gives the order to storm the castle, but he and his brave knights are forced to retreat after being bombarded by a further array of farmyard animals.

The quest seems doomed to fail but Sir Bedevere, however, has a cunning plan, and he, Arthur, and the other knights disappear into the surrounding woodland. The French guards appear mystified by the sound of extensive carpentry that fills the night air, and so imagine their surprise when the coming dawn brings not only daylight but also a gift in the form of a forty-foot high wooden rabbit, which has a bright red bow tied around its neck, and a card bearing the greeting 'Pour votre amis Français' (for our French friends).

It is while the bewildered guards are hauling the gigantic rabbit into the castle that Sir Bedevere reveals his plan, which would see himself, Sir Lancelot and Sir Galahad waiting until nightfall before leaping out of the rabbit and taking the castle. Arthur sighs in dismay and Sir Bedevere, who has also realised the tiny (but devastatingly fatal) flaw in the plan, suggests that they might build a large wooden badger. Arthur is about to berate his comrade but falls into silence as a loud twanging noise fills the air. Once again he and the knights are forced to retreat as the wooden rabbit comes hurtling over the battlements, killing yet another unfortunate page.

Trivia Fact: This scene was also filmed at Doune Castle, but instead of using the actual castle the production crew built a false six-foot wall atop a hill at the rear of the castle. The camera was then positioned so that it pointed up the hill to give the impression of height.

The scene cuts to a crusty old Oxford-type professor, whose name was apparently 'Frank', posing for the camera outside the castle (filmed at

Arnhall Castle, near Stirling). Frank waits for his cue before informing his unseen audience of how the ferocity of the French taunting had taken Arthur by surprise, and that in order for Arthur to succeed in his quest to find the Grail he would now need to find a new strategy. But just as the learned Frank is about to reveal that strategy, which would involve the knights separating and searching for the Grail individually, the historian is hacked down by a mounted knight who then disappears off camera. The historian's wife, who was probably only there in a show of support for her husband, is clearly distraught at the sudden turn of events on what was supposed to be nothing more than a short educational film on medieval Britain. She naturally calls the police who arrive at the scene and open up their murder investigation.

The first knight that we follow in search of the Grail is Sir Robin, who is being regaled in song by his ever-faithful band of musicians. Our not-so-brave knight is at first pleased with the wording of the ditty, but quickly calls a halt to the merriment when the lute player sings a verse detailing gruesome injuries such as having "his liver removed, and his bowels unplugged", and "his nostrils raped, and his bottom burnt off".

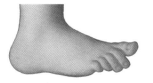

Trivia Fact: The horse upon which the historian-murdering knight is mounted is the only real horse seen in the movie. (The reason perhaps being that this was the only nag in Scotland with an 'equinity card'.)

Sir Robin's fragile nerve is further stretched as he and his men happen upon three dead knights, each of whom is impaled upon a single lance protruding from a tree. Oh how he must have been wishing that he had paid more heed to the signpost which warned travellers (in triplicate) that certain death lay but one mile ahead, and that this particular path was for 'dead people only'. It is while he is pondering whether to turn back that he and his men are confronted by a monstrous three-headed knight who, upon learning that Sir Robin is a Knight of the Round Table, refuses to allow him to pass and then begins arguing amongst itself as to whether it should kill Sir Robin before or after having tea and biscuits. Fortunately for our cowardly hero, the three-way bickering allows him ample time to beat a hasty retreat, an act that unfortunately does not go unnoticed by his merry band.

We now go in search of Sir Galahad and his quest to find the Grail, which, when we join our hero, appears illuminated in the night sky above the foreboding Castle Anthrax in the distance. Upon entering the castle, our brave knight is met by Zoot (played by Python stalwart Carol Cleveland), and two vestal virgin types called Midget and Crapper – which must have confused Sir Galahad as neither girl appeared stunted or incontinent. Zoot mildly scolds Sir Galahad for

appearing so ungallant as to refuse such warm and friendly hospitality before going on to inform him that the Castle Anthrax is home to eight score young blondes and brunettes, all aged between sixteen and nineteen, and all of whom seem resigned to a life spent bathing, dressing, undressing and making exciting underwear, and who are feeling somewhat neglected.

Sir Galahad refuses to allow himself to be distracted, and after ignoring medical advice from Drs Piglet and Winston, he sets forth to search the castle for the Grail, but is soon halted in his tracks upon entering a chamber which is filled with the aforementioned eight score blondes and brunettes. It is here that our 'chaste' knight encounters Zoot's identical twin sister 'Dingo' (Cleveland again), who informs Sir Galahad that the grail which he espied from yonder afar is not the actual Grail at all but rather a grail-shaped beacon that her naughty sister had lit to lure unsuspecting knights to the castle. Alas and woe for Sir Galahad, but not, however, for Python aficionados, for it is here that the previously-omitted scene is restored to its former glory – and even if one should fail to spot the extra footage, Zoot comes to the rescue by turning to the camera and enquiring as to whether the scene should have been cut in the first place. When all is said and done, the additional twenty-four seconds is little more than a montage of various characters (including the left head of the three-headed knight and the socialist militant 'Dennis') commenting on the restored scene's merits.

Dingo, sensing Sir Galahad's disappointment, insists that her sister must be punished for having set the beacon alight and there is but one punishment for such a heinous crime; she will have to be tied down and spanked. The retribution does not end there, however,

Trivia Fact: Palin plays the most parts in the movie – ten in all.

for once he has finished spanking Zoot, he must then spank Dingo, and then there are the three nymphets standing beside Dingo, aptly named 'Amazing', 'Stunner' and 'Lovely', who also insist on being spanked before then partaking in the 'oral sex'.

Sir Galahad, up until this point, has been attempting to take his leave but upon hearing of this mouth-watering prospect he admits that he could stay a little while longer. But the knight's night of sordid sex is cruelly snatched away from him as Sir Lancelot comes to his supposed rescue. Sir Lancelot believes he has saved his comrade in arms from a deadly peril and is unwilling to listen to Sir Galahad's insistence that it is his duty as a Knight of the Round Table to sample as much peril as possible. But, alas, his pleas fall on deaf ears, and he accuses Sir Lancelot of being gay.

In a continuity error, when Sir Lancelot and Sir Galahad have exited the castle and are making their way along the wall, a crew member can be spotted, albeit briefly, on camera (keep watching the left of your screen) – although, to be fair to the Pythons, in one scene of *Ben Hur* there is a chariot rider wearing a wristwatch!

Meanwhile, King Arthur and Sir Bedevere, who are but an unladen swallow's flight away, encounter an old man who informs them that in order to find the Grail they must first seek out 'Tim the Enchanter', who knows of a cave which no man has ever entered. Beyond the cave which no man has ever entered is the Bridge of Death, which spans the Gorge of Eternal Peril, which no man has apparently crossed... hee, hee, hee, hee, hee, ha, ha, ha...

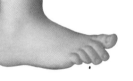

Trivia Fact: According to Michael Palin in the DVD commentary of *Holy Grail*, the word 'Ni!' was derived from *The Goon Show*.

It is while Arthur and Bedevere are seeking out the Enchanter, who will lead them to the cave, which no man... etc., etc., that they happen upon the Knights Who Say 'Ni!', who are the keepers of the apparently sacred words 'Ni', 'Peng' and 'Neee-wom'. In order for Arthur and Bedevere to pass, they must first perform a task to appease the Knights Who Say 'Ni!', and momentarily put their quest for the Grail on hold while they set forth to obtain, of all things, a shrubbery – one that is nice, and not too expensive. By the time Arthur and Sir Bedevere return with the finest-looking shrubbery they can find at such notice, they discover that the Knights Who Say 'Ni!' no longer say 'Ni!' at all, and are now the Knights Who Say 'Ecky, ecky, ecky, ecky, pikang, zoop, boing, goodem, zoo, owli, zhiv'. The newly named knights then set Arthur a second test – yes, you've guessed it – to find another shrubbery (only one that is slightly higher than the first, in order to

achieve a two-level effect with a nice path running down the middle). But that's not all – for once Arthur and Sir Bedevere have succeeded in finding a second shrubbery, they must then cut down the mightiest tree in the forest with – "a herring!"

And so we come to the tale of Sir Lancelot, but before we meet up with the brave (and possibly gay) knight, we must first enter Swamp Castle (Doune Castle again) where a decidedly delicate (and almost *certainly* gay) Prince Herbert (Jones) is being lectured to, on what we soon learn is his wedding day, by his overbearing father (Palin) who stands proudly pointing towards the window informing his son that all that he surveys will one day be his.

"What, the curtains?" enquires the sullen prince.

"No, not the curtains, lad," replies the exasperated king in a broad Yorkshire accent. "All that you can see, stretched out over the hills and valleys of this land."

When the dainty prince expresses his reluctance, his father embarks on a hilarious monologue of how he had built the kingdom up from nothing, and how other kings had called him insane for deciding to build his castle on a swamp. The original castle had sunk into the swamp, but the king remained undeterred and had built a second castle that had also apparently sunk beneath the mire. The third castle went the same way as its two predecessors, but not before having burnt down and fallen over. The fourth castle, however, and the one in which they are now standing, has remained upright, and it is this – the strongest castle in the land – that he, Prince Herbert, will surely inherit. Unfortunately for the king, his son confesses that he has no interest in anything other than singing, but just as the prince is about to burst into song, his father turns to the camera and calls a halt to the proceedings and insists that his son will go ahead with his wedding to Princess Lucky, who is apparently beautiful, rich and has huge "tracts of land". So he'd just better "shut his noise" and "get his suit on" – and "no singing!"

As Sir Lancelot is approaching Swamp Castle, his trusty page Concorde (Idle) is struck by an arrow containing a message of distress from Prince Herbert. Sir Lancelot reads the message, which he believes could lead him to the Grail, and before setting off towards the castle he assures brave Concorde that he will not have died in vain. When Concorde insists that he is neither dying, nor mortally wounded, and that he is in fact up to the task of accompanying his master, Sir Lancelot in turn insists that the sweet Concorde should remain where he lay and rest until he himself has accomplished a daring and heroic rescue in his own particular... idiom.

Sir Lancelot then storms the castle single-handedly and slaughters several guards, which allegedly cost the king £50 each, and also eight wedding guests – including the bride's father – until he at last stands before the prince, whom he had believed to be a princess. The king is naturally upset by this upturn in events, but his anger soon diminishes upon learning that Sir Lancelot hails from Camelot, which is a very nice castle, and apparently situated within "good pig country". (In a continuity error, one of the guards that Sir Lancelot has killed can be spotted waving to the camera!)

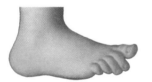

Trivia Fact: A young Iain Banks, later to become the award-winning and prolific author of Complicity and The Wasp Factory, among many others, can be seen as an extra in the film. He was a student at Stirling University at the time.

All the while, Prince Herbert has been otherwise engaged in securing a homemade rope to the bed-frame, with which he and Sir Lancelot can make their escape down the castle wall. Unfortunately for the prince, the homemade rope fails to support his weight and we hear him cry out as he plummets to his death. But this is a mere technicality to the king, as is the killing of the best man, and someone else's auntie, and he sets out to marry Princess Lucky to the brave, if somewhat dangerous, Sir Lancelot. The king's new plan, however, appears to be ruined when his supposedly dead son enters the chamber and threatens to break into song to reveal how he had come to be saved at the last minute. The king once again attempts to stop his son from singing, but the surviving guests seem intent on hearing the prince's song. Fortunately for Sir Lancelot, Concorde arrives in the nick of time and beckons for his master to follow him, but this means of escape isn't right for Sir Lancelot's 'idiom' – as he feels it needs to be more 'dramatic'.

In another continuity error, after Sir Lancelot has wreaked havoc on the wedding party, the bride, Princess Lucky, is first shown with no blood on her face. On the next close-up, however, blood is seen pouring from her mouth and running down her chin – and in the next shot the blood has vanished again.

Arthur and Sir Bedevere, who have refused to seek out another shrubbery, or attempt to fell a tree with the aforementioned herring, have been reunited with Sir Robin, and the three set forth across the land in search of Tim the Enchanter. Beyond the forest they are reunited with Sir Lancelot and Sir Galahad, and there is much rejoicing, but the rejoicing ends amid the frozen land of Nador, where they are forced to eat the minstrels.

A year passes. Winter changes into spring (mmm), and spring into summer (ahh), but then summer changes back into winter (oh?), and winter then gives spring and summer amiss and goes straight into autumn. Until one day...

Arthur and his band of knights happen upon Tim the Enchanter (Cleese), a man who can not only summon up fire without flint or tinder, but can also help them in their quest to find the Grail. Tim tells Arthur to ride north, for there they will find the Cave of Caerbannog, wherein, carved in mystic runes upon the rock, are the last words of Olfin Bedwere of Rheged, which apparently make plain the last resting place of the elusive Grail. But Tim warns Arthur that only men of valour should enter the cave, for it is guarded by a creature so foul, that the bones of fifty men lay strewn about its lair, and that death awaits them with "nasty, big, pointy teeth".

Trivia Fact: The cave used for this scene is a Nineteenth Century copper mine situated near Loch Tay, and was the same one used in Alfred Hitchcock's *Thirty-Nine Steps*.

Upon reaching the cave, Arthur can't believe what he is seeing when 'death with nasty, big, pointy teeth' appears to be nothing more than a harmless-looking white bunny rabbit. Sir Robin chastises Tim for having scared him so much that he'd "soiled his armour", and Arthur ignores Tim's warnings and casually orders Bors (Gilliam) to chop the rabbit's head off. When the murderous rabbit decapitates the unsuspecting Bors, Arthur orders a full charge, for he is King of the Britons, and therefore fears no man-dibles (cue audible groan).

There follows a brief, yet extremely ferocious, fight scene during which Gawain and another unnamed knight are also slain by the rabbit before Arthur orders a retreat. Sir Robin suggests that they should run away some more in order to confuse the rabbit, but

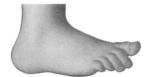

Trivia Fact: The idea for the 'killer rabbit' was taken from the façade of the Notre Dame cathedral in Paris. At the cathedral's entrance there is a series of panels, each depicting man's infirmities. 'Cowardice' shows an armoured knight fleeing from a rabbit.

Trivia Fact: The original script called for the Grail to be discovered in Harrods, the famous store located in Knightsbridge, London – although one piece of Python legend/trivia does make claim to the fact that they had gone so far over budget in Scotland, that they could hardly afford to travel back to London just to shoot one scene! When asked, years later, by author David Morgan whether he had learned anything from the Holy Grail experience, Eric Idle replied: "Always have sufficient budget. Try and stay out of soggy woollen armour."

Arthur knows that the cave contains clues as to the Grail's resting place, and they must enter at all costs. He therefore calls upon Brother Maynard (Palin), the keeper of the sacred relics, to bring forth the Holy Hand-Grenade of Antioch.

In yet another continuity error, during the assault on the rabbit the knights drop their shields. Sir Galahad drops his in front of the cave's entrance, but in the next shot the shield is back on his arm. When the knights return to the entrance, all the shields have vanished.

Brother Maynard is forced to consult the *Book of Armaments*, which contains the Lord's instructions on how to detonate the device. Once the rabbit has been dispatched to the celestial rabbit hutch in the sky, Arthur and the surviving knights enter the cave. As Brother Maynard is also a scholar, he is called upon to decipher the ancient text carved upon the cave wall, which reads: "Here may be found the last words of Joseph of Arimathea. He who is valiant and pure of spirit may find the Grail in the Castle of Aaaaagggh..."

(When the knights were reading the text, their gaze should have moved from right-to-left, as this is how Aramaic was written.)

There then follows a silly debate as to the true meaning of 'Aaaaagggh', and it is Brother Maynard who once again proves his worth by solving the puzzle in that 'Aaaaagggh' was actually the 'Beast of Aaauugh'. At that moment the dreaded animated beast attacks and eats Brother Maynard, but thankfully Arthur and the others manage to escape when the animator (Gilliam) suffers a fatal heart attack.

The cartoon peril is no more. The quest for the Grail can continue...

And so Arthur and his intrepid knights arrive at the Bridge of Death (filmed near the area known as the 'Meeting of the Three Waters' in Glen Coe), which is guarded by the Bridgekeeper (Gilliam), also known as 'the old man from scene twenty four', who will ask them five (three, sire, three) questions, and only those who answer all three questions correctly may cross in safety. Sir Robin, upon learning that anyone getting a question wrong will be cast into the 'Gorge of Eternal Peril', refuses to participate in this deadly game of Trivial Pursuit, and when he is ordered to do so by his king, he cunningly suggests that the ever-so-more-brave Sir Lancelot should go first.

Sir Lancelot steps up to the Bridgekeeper and, after supplying information such as his name, his quest and that his favourite colour is blue, is allowed to cross. Sir Robin, realising that the questions are but simple ones, rushes forward and casually supplies his name and his quest, but is cast into the gorge for failing to know the capital of Assyria.

Sir Galahad is also cast into the gorge for having failed to realise that his favourite colour was actually yellow and not blue. One would have expected Sir Bedevere the 'Wise' to accept the Bridgekeeper's challenge, but it is Arthur who steps forward and, upon being asked the air-speed velocity of an unladen swallow, flummoxes the Bridgekeeper by asking him if he is referring to an African or European swallow. The Bridgekeeper is cast down into the gorge, which allows Arthur and Sir Bedevere to cross unhindered.

Sadly, there is no sign of Sir Lancelot (who has probably been arrested as part of the on-going investigation into Frank the Historian's murder), but the duo do not despair for long, for they see Castle Aaaaagggh (Castle Stalker) standing upon a tiny island amid a vast lake. They engage the services of the local boatkeeper to ferry them to the island, but as Arthur is giving thanks to God for having guided them thus far, a dead sheep comes vaulting over the castle's parapet and almost kills him.

Much to Arthur's dismay, he discovers that the castle is occupied by the French, including the same guard (Cleese), who had taunted him so mercilessly previously. Arthur is furious that the French have dared to profane the castle with their presence and demands that they open the doors to him, but is taunted again with the guard threatening to

Trivia Fact: The Bridge of Death scene was actually the first scene to be filmed, but Chapman, a chronic alcoholic, was apparently so drunk that he was unable to walk across, and so they had to use a stand-in (the first assistant director).

Trivia Fact: As the gorge spanned some seventy feet across, and was one hundred feet deep, the Glen Coe Mountain Rescue Team stood in for the Pythons cast into its maw.

Trivia Fact: The dead sheep used in the scene was an actual dead sheep that the production crew happened upon in a nearby field. Fortunately for Chapman, the sheep had been gutted first, but would still have been of considerable weight.

Spamalot

Monty Python's *Spamalot* is a comedic musical based on the film *Monty Python and the Holy Grail*. Like the film, it is a highly irreverent and very silly mockery of Arthurian legend, but it differs from the film in many other ways, especially its parodies of Broadway theatre. Eric Idle, a member of the Monty Python team, wrote the musical's book and lyrics, and collaborated with John Du Prez on the music. It was directed by Mike Nichols, and won the Tony Award for Best Musical of the 2004-2005 season.

Spamalot's plot follows King Arthur as he journeys to find the Holy Grail. Arthur, travelling with his servant Patsy, recruits several knights to accompany him on his quest, including Sir Robin, Sir Lancelot and Sir Galahad. Along the way, they meet the Lady of the Lake and a host of other odd characters, including Prince Herbert, the French Taunter, Tim the Enchanter, the Black Knight and the Knights Who Say 'Ni!'

The original cast includes Tim Curry as King Arthur, Michael McGrath as Patsy, David Hyde Pierce as Sir Robin, Hank Azaria as Sir Lancelot and other roles (including the French Taunter and Tim the Enchanter), Christopher Sieber as Sir Galahad, and Sara Ramirez as the Lady of the Lake. It also includes Christian Borle as Prince Herbert and John Cleese as the (recorded) voice of God. The original production has been both a financial and critical success. *Variety* reported advance ticket sales of $18 million, with ticket prices ranging from $36 to $101.

Monty Python fans appreciate its many references to the film and other material in the Python canon, including a line from the 'Lumberjack Song', nods to the 'Ministry of Silly Walks', the 'Election Night Special' and 'Parrot' routines, a rendition of the song 'Always Look on the Bright Side of Life' from the film *Monty Python's Life of Brian*, and the 'Fish Schlapping Song' which

fire arrows at the top of the English k-nnniggets' heads, and make castanets out of their testicles. He also intends to unclog his nose in Arthur's direction whilst waving his private parts at the king's aunties.

Against a backdrop of stirring music Arthur draws Excalibur and, after declaring that this day will be the day that the blood of many an English knight will be avenged, orders the charge. At first it appears that only he and Sir Bedevere will be making the charge, but it is then that a vast army (of extras, consisting of the local populace and students from the nearby Stirling University) suddenly appears upon the shore ready to do the aforementioned avenging. The blood of many an English knight appears destined to remain unavenged, however, when the charge is thwarted by the untimely arrival of the local constabulary, who burst onto the scene amidst wailing sirens. Both Arthur and Sir Bedevere are arrested not merely for carrying offensive weapons, but also for Frank's murder after having been identified by the slain historian's wife; this signifies the end of the movie.

In the years since the movie, *Grail* is now the only Python movie to produce a full set of Python action figures (there's a small number of *Brian* ones, but not a full set).

In 2005, the Broadway musical *Spamalot* (a version of *Grail* re-written by Eric Idle and John Du Prez, and directed by 'A'-list Hollywood film director Mike Nichols) opened to incredible box office success. Python re-unions these days are few and far between, but the five remaining principal players all made it to Manhattan for opening night. A London production of *Spamalot* will be opening at the Palace Theatre on 2 October 2006. The United States national tour of the musical will begin on 7 March 2006 at the Colonial Theater in Boston,

Massachusetts. Starting in 2007, a production of the musical will reside for ten years at a Wynn Las Vegas theatre being built specifically for the show.

is a reference to both 'The Fish-Slapping Dance' and the song 'Finland'.

Broadway musical fans appreciate its visual and auditory references to other musicals and musical theatre in general, such as 'The Song That Goes Like This' (a spoof of Andrew Lloyd Webber productions and many other Broadway power ballads), the knights doing a dance reminiscent of *Fiddler on the Roof*, the Laker Girls doing a dance reminiscent of *West Side Story* (complete with music), Azaria's mimicking of Peter Allen in 'His Name Is Lancelot', the character of Sir Not Appearing in This Show being *Don Quixote* and a line pulled from 'Another Hundred People' from Sondheim's *Company* by the 'damsel' Herbert. The song 'You Won't Succeed (On Broadway)' also parodies *The Producers*, *Yentl* and other Jewish-related shows.

The original Broadway production received fourteen Tony Award nominations, more than any other show in the 2004-2005 season. It won three of them: Best Musical, Best Performance by a Featured Actress in a Musical (Sara Ramirez) and Best Direction of a Musical (Mike Nichols).

– From *Wikipedia.com*

CHAPTER FIVE:
MONTY PYTHON LIVE!

Immanuel Kant was a real pissant
Who was very rarely stable,
Heidegger, Heidegger was a
Boozy beggar
Who could think you under
The table.

Putting the successful television series onto the stage was first mentioned in 1973. The idea had been to start with a West End run in London, but on making enquires into this the answer that came back was that the minimum West End run was three months, and due to successful solo projects nobody actually had three months' time in one block to give to the project. In February 1974, however, the Monty Python team opened a short run at the Theatre Royal, Drury Lane in London. This performance was culled from classic TV show sketches, a bunch of songs by Neil Innes and the resurrection of a few Cleese/Chapman sketches dating back to *At Last the 1948 Show* and *Cambridge Circus*. The show also resulted in the now famous Charisma Records album *Monty Python Live at Drury Lane*; during the 'Parrot' sketch the audience can be heard clearly shouting out every line, not unlike a rock audience singing along.

We were convinced Python wouldn't go in America. We were so convinced that when they asked us to buy the format for US television, we turned them down, just to piss them off! (Eric Idle)

Perhaps the finest live moment ever for the Pythons must surely be their concerts at the Hollywood Bowl. The shows were filmed and became the now-legendary comedy DVD *Monty Python Live at the Hollywood Bowl*, which must surely be the stopgap for every American comedy fan between Richard Pryor and *The Simpsons*. In the years prior to their American stage triumph, Monty Python had risen to

Trivia Fact: On the original vinyl version of *Live at Drury Lane*, Eric Idle mentions the chocolate bar 'Breakaway' during the 'Nudge Nudge' sketch. He did, of course, use this sketch to advertise the biscuit, but on later vinyl and CD versions this 'plug' is missing.

God-like status following an initial US cult television start. After *Life of Brian*, they took their newfound rock star status and filled the 15,000 capacity Bowl on not one but five nights (although the first night was an open dress rehearsal, they still sold the place out). In comedy terms this was unheard of; the only people who performed five nights at the Bowl were rock groups (in the Sixties, the Beatles had the house record for ticket sales).

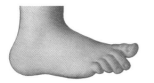

Trivia Fact: When Monty Python signed their album deal with Charisma Records, they assumed it was completed after they handed in the soundtrack to *Life of Brian*, only to be informed, like the Beatles before them, that film soundtracks don't actually count. It was after hearing this news that they completed one final studio album, entitled, fittingly, *Contractual Obligation*.

This new live show, presented between 25 and 29 September 1980, was a mix of old television sketches, more obscure sketches, some earlier pre-Python moments and a chance to give some of the material from their recent *Contractual Obligation* album an airing before a live audience. They were, of course, joined by Neil Innes and Carol Cleveland. Esteemed comedy writer Robert Ross called the show "a collection of the most important and hilarious sketches of the post-war years". It was high praise indeed, and one viewing of the DVD will prove this show to be the Monty Python team at their live best – sheer comedy perfection captured on film.

When Ron Devillier finally put it out in Dallas – and it always amused us that it started in Dallas of all places – all his pals were ringing him up saying, "Have they burned the station down last night?" or "Did they stone you on your way to work?" And the moment Ron said it was fine, they all started putting it out. (John Cleese)

Some of the sketches performed at the Hollywood Bowl were slightly changed for the benefit of an American audience; for instance, in the 'Football World Forum' sketch Teddy Johnson and Pearl Carr become Jerry Lee Lewis, while Neil Innes also includes his Bonzo Dog Doo-Dah Band hit 'I'm the Urban Spaceman' because the audience would already be very familiar with it. As in the UK years, the audience also knew the words pretty much verbatim and can be heard and seen quite easily chanting along like a sing-a-long rock crowd.

The shows were booked as something of a 'break' between *Life of Brian* and *Meaning of Life*. After thirteen solid weeks of script writing and many full script reading sessions, they possibly felt like a pleasant break too! There was also a chance to generate some incredibly quick cash, a fact that wouldn't have gone unnoticed by Denis O'Brian, George Harrison's business partner at Handmade Films, the company responsible for making the movie version.

When Holy Grail *came out, we came over and did some publicity for that, and it was a very different sort of feeling. We sort of felt, "Yes, our audience had found us," totally different from the Joey Bishop/Johnny Carson audience. And of course in the States it's a big enough audience to make a difference.* (Terry Jones)

An earlier US appearance by the Python team is also available on CD as *Monty Python Live at City Center* (Arista Records AB 4073). These recordings were culled from shows between 14 April and 2 May 1976, and produced by music business PR director Nancy Lewis, who later became Python's US manager for a short time. At the time of their performances at the Hollywood Bowl (1980), the Pythons were indeed in the middle of writing material for their next movie, although by the time they reached the Hollywood stage it was no more than a bunch of sketches. These were set anywhere between 1880 and 1980. At this point in time, John Cleese informed the rest of the team that they should use all the material they had written and make a groundbreaking sketch movie, but the rest of the group thought that this would be little more than backtracking after the plot-driven storylines of both *Grail* and *Brian*.

It was fantastic; we were like rock stars. What's so weird about it, [is that] it was at a time when becoming a rock star was a dream – everybody wanted to be a rock star. And we kind of did it in a different way. It wasn't like we set out to do it; but we ended up on those American tours, and it

Trivia Fact: One of the items to be found in the Hollywood Bowl programme was a fold-out poster which included a Terry Gilliam drawing of 'Bruce', along with the words to 'Philosopher's Song'. These items now command a decent price on eBay; pity no one involved had the foresight that they might, because at sound checks some days the team could be found making paper planes out of the vast amount of 'spares' they printed!

Trivia Fact: According to press speculation, the Monty Python team were due to re-unite for a number of US live stage shows in 2001, although these turned out to be little more than newspaper gossip.

was like that. Having Hollywood Bowl with 15,000 people sitting out there doing lines with you, it was good fun. (Terry Gilliam)

In 1988, the US cable television network HBO held its comedy awards show in Aspen, Colorado. What made this show more legendary than any before it was the fact that the five remaining Pythons would appear together in order to accept their lifetime achievement award. Eddie Izzard (who had taken the prize for best stand-up comedian that night) began the show on 7 March by trying to upstage the Pythons and collect their award himself, but this confusion was soon blown over by the arrival to the stage of the gentlemen known as Palin, Jones, Idle, Cleese and Gilliam, with (of course) an urn, supposedly containing the remains of Chapman, and placed on an empty sixth seat.

The events of this evening are available to view on DVD on both sides of the Atlantic under the title *Monty Python Live at Aspen*, and while the bulk of the show is a large bunch of clips, commented on later by various members of the team, there is also some hilarious new material, including Graham's ashes ending up on the floor while Michael and John both run for an off-stage vacuum cleaner. It's pure Python. The climax is an Eric Idle-led audience sing a-long with all the usual favourites, including a rousing version of *Always Look on the Bright Side of Life*.

There was a sleazy club in downtown Manhattan that called itself Monty Python's Flying Circus. We couldn't believe it. Then they went out of business, and we started getting odd bills, things they hadn't paid!
(Nancy Lewis, music industry promoter who first brought Python to the US)

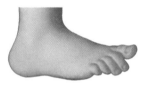

Trivia Fact: When Eric Idle made the movie *The Rutles: All You Need is Cash*, ex-Beatle George Harrison made an appearance as a TV reporter. John Lennon is also said to have loved the movie.

After Aspen the Pythons returned to being solo players. Both television and the big screen called, and this pulled the five of them into different directions, though they are often reunited. Take the 1996 production of *Wind in the Willows*, written by Terry Jones and starring both himself and Eric Idle, with John Cleese and Michael Palin in smaller roles. The film was produced by John Goldstone, and featured songs written by John Du Prez, Andre Jacquemin, Terry Jones and Dave Howman – so, short of being Python in all but name, it was Python in all but Gilliam! To celebrate their thirtieth anniversary in 1999, the BBC2 television channel handed the Pythons an entire Saturday evening to do with as they wished. The outcome was a number of documentaries, most notably *It's the Monty Python Story*, held together by a bunch of brand new sketches performed by Terry Jones, Michael Palin, John Cleese and Terry Gilliam, although Eric Idle did take part in the interviews and documentaries from his home in LA.

CHAPTER SIX:
THE LIFE OF BRIAN

And he started to shave
And have one off the wrist,
And want to see girls
And go out and get pissed...
A man called 'Brian',
This man called 'Brian',
The man they called 'Brian',
This man called 'Brian!'

The 2004 DVD single-disc release contains the usual extras such as 'Scene Selections', 'Subtitles', 'Movie Trailers', etc., but what will be of particular interest to Python aficionados is 'The Python Trailers' – an on-location BBC documentary, somewhere in Tunisia, circa 1979 AD, which sees the six Pythons discussing each other, their solo projects and, of course, *Life of Brian*.

The documentary begins with the team in full costume reading the script from the 'What Have the Romans Ever Done for Us?' scene, while the BBC voiceover informs the viewer how it had been ten years since the Pythons first got together in 1969, how the team had made forty-five episodes of *Monty Python's Flying Circus*, which were sold to over twenty countries, (cue brief snippet of a German-dubbed 'Lumberjack Song'), and that they had seen their last movie, *Holy Grail*, grossing some $10,000,000.

In the five years since *Grail*, the individual Python members had had varying degrees of success. Cleese had received great acclaim for two series of *Fawlty Towers*, which were commissioned by the BBC; Palin and Jones had their *Ripping Yarns*, also commissioned by the BBC; Idle had *Rutland Weekend Television*, and its subsequent spin-off *The Rutles*, a Beatles-esque parody which George Harrison and John Lennon both apparently liked, as did Ringo Starr, but only after '68. Chapman had written, directed and starred in *The Odd-Job Man* (1978), while Gilliam had directed *Jabberwocky*, which also starred Palin.

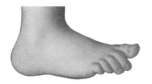

Trivia Fact: On New Year's Day 2006, Stephen Fry hosted *The 50 Greatest Comedy Films* on Channel 4 TV in the UK, voted for by the British public. The number one movie of the night was *Life of Brian*.

By this time, however, somewhere in Tunisia, and many miles from EMI's Manchester Square, London offices, a dedicated crew was busy transforming a small stretch of desert into Judea, but without EMI's cash it seemed that their efforts would be in vain. Although the Pythons successfully sued EMI, settling out of court, the team needed to find alternative funding, and with the cameras waiting to roll, they needed to find it fast. Convinced that the team wouldn't find the necessary financial backing in the UK, Eric Idle accompanied producer John Goldstone to Hollywood. Upon learning that the ex-Beatle and renowned Python aficionado George Harrison was in town, Idle approached him. Harrison not only agreed to step in at the eleventh hour; he even set up his own company, 'Handmade Films', for the project. (When he first thought of the company name, Harrison coined 'British Handmade Films', which his business partner Denis O'Brian instantly dismissed because, "anything named 'British' these days is doomed to lose money!"). When asked why he had done so, Harrison replied "because I wanted to see the film", which isn't a bad reason, is it? This was the second time in as many years that EMI succeeded in shooting itself in the financial foot by electing to jump upon the blasphemy bandwagon and withdraw financial backing from a movie which would go on to be voted the greatest comedy film of all time in a 2000 readers' poll conducted by *Total Film* magazine, and the fifth greatest British film of all time by the magazine in 2004. The first shooting occurred when the corporation announced its decision to drop the UK's then-hottest group, the Sex Pistols, from its roster within three months of having signed the group, over fears of a public backlash against the group's supposed outrageous behaviour.

CHAPTER SIX

After the initial quip in New York at the opening of Grail, *Gilliam and I got drunk in Amsterdam and began to make bad-taste carpenter jokes, about JC (Jack Christ not Jesus Cleese!), and him being nailed inadequately to a cross by a poor workman, and trying to give the carpenters advice since they were so bad. And the cross kept falling over and he went slap face first in the mud – those sort of sophomoric gags which are hilarious when you are in a nice warm bar in Amsterdam with several bottles of Dutch beer inside you.* (Eric Idle)

The six Pythons appear in good humour and are happy to praise their former colleagues' solo successes, but are also equally happy to denigrate each other, which I suppose is only to be expected from five former 'Oxbridge' graduates with degrees in satirical wit, and an equally-zany American whose life seems to be divided into two categories: things which are "great", and others that "piss him off".

Chapman not only talks openly about his homosexuality (whilst a young dark-skinned beauty is sitting on his lap), his former dependency on alcohol (he'd finally beat the bottle two years earlier in 1977), but also about how meeting the Queen Mother, whilst he was the secretary of the Student Union at St Bartholomew's College, had led to his decision to turn his back on a career in medicine and go on a tour of New Zealand and America with the Cambridge Footlights troupe.

Cleese talks candidly about his decision to "run away from" the circus, which was mainly due to his having spent ten months of every year, for five years, with Python, and that he'd felt it was time to go off and "chase his own tail". He's also happy to divulge his fellow Pythons' idiosyncrasies, which include Idle's incessant need to tell jokes for hours upon end, Jones' fanaticism for all things under the sun (and how it was best to avoid getting into an argument with the Welshman unless one had a free week), Gilliam's limited vocabulary and Palin for being appallingly "normal", and "too nice for his own good", before going on to describe his old friend as a "creative genius". He also talks about his decidedly dodgy looking hair-weave, porcelain teeth and tax-deductible knee joints (well, this is Python, after all).

Trivia Fact: Spike Milligan had been holidaying in Tunisia at the time of filming, and so when the Pythons heard that the former 'Goon' was staying close by, they offered him a part in the movie.

Palin claims that Cleese is a "strange fellow", who's so tall that his head is permanently lost in the clouds, whilst he's also "tender", "shy" and, oh yes, he apparently takes sex too seriously. Gilliam discusses his decision to step aside and give Jones free reign to direct alone, on the premise that in the case of movie directing, two heads are not necessarily better than one.

I remember Eric coming up with Jesus Christ: Lust for Glory. *What a wonderful, wonderful title. How do you put a film to that? We knew we needed to work in an area which would stimulate us and which would be different from anything we'd done before, and would be, in a sense, quite abrasive. And religion was something I think we all had very similar views about: We had all been spoon fed it in large, regular doses when we were young and yet none of us were religious now, so what was going on? What were the mistakes? So the idea of doing a film about religion was really intriguing. But how do you do it, how you make it funny, so it's not just amazingly dull?* (Michael Palin)

We are also given an interesting insight as to how the team has once again divided into their former two-man cliques, with Chapman and Cleese sharing one trailer, Palin and Jones in another and Idle and Gilliam sharing the third.

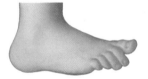

Trivia Fact: When *Life of Brian* was granted a theatrical release in Sweden, some Abba-loving, Volvo-driving Swedish marketing executive came up with the idea to 'get one over' on his Scandinavian neighbour by advertising it as "the movie that was so funny it was banned in Norway".

There are also interviews with Spike Milligan, who plays the role of the 'Mad Prophet', and Python stalwart Carol Cleveland, as well as a plethora of clips from *Monty Python's Flying Circus*, such as 'Upper-class Twit of the Year', 'Fish-Slapping Dance' and 'The Marriage Guidance Counsellor', along with clips from *Fawlty Towers, Rutland Weekend Television, Ripping Yarns, The Odd-Job Man* and *Jabberwocky.* Life of Brian *was great, smart and a very funny movie.* (John Landis)

Upon its release in 1979, *Life of Brian*, perhaps not surprisingly given the movie's subject matter, immediately created a storm of controversy, with the Roman Catholic Church going so far as to condemn the movie as 'blasphemous' – much to the obvious delight of the Python team. Countries where Catholicism was the predominant faith, such as Ireland, Italy and Spain, all announced a total blanket ban on the movie, which led to it becoming something of a cult classic amongst the younger, more liberal-thinking generations of those countries. The Norwegian government was equally quick to impose a ban on the movie, which lasted some twelve months, on the grounds that it was 'too blasphemous'. (It took eight years for the movie to be released in Ireland; it wasn't released in Italy until the Nineties, with no word that it was made in 1979; the film was so popular that *And Now for Something Completely Different* was subsequently released in the country.)

I remember getting to the crucifixion period, thinking, "How on Earth do we do this?" And I said, "Let's apply the same rule: Let's just look at the historical background." The historical background is that Jesus' crucifixion was not a unique event, it was part of a regular entertainment that was put on by the Romans both to impress their power and authority and to entertain people – you know, people would be crucified and there would also be fairs: bread and circuses and crucifixions. Once you accept that it wasn't a unique event, then you can begin to introduce characters who would have been around then, like the terribly decent man who offers to take the cross and the guy just runs off. (Michael Palin)

The hardest thing in a comedy film is to work the balance between plot and comedy, and here the balance works. (Charlie Higson on *Brian*)

The movie also came under fire in Britain, where leaders from both the Church of England and the Catholic Church were outraged, and accused Messrs Chapman, Cleese, Gilliam, Idle, Jones and Palin of mocking Christianity itself. If, however, any of those religious zealots, who were calling for the movie to be banned, had bothered to go along to their local cinema they would have seen for themselves that the Python team were not attempting to get cheap laughs by lambasting Jesus Christ, but had simply used their collective comedy genius to make a movie which is actually parodying that period of time, whilst satirically attacking the political and religious tensions in the Middle East.

In fact, this revealing truism comes very early on in the movie when the narrator points out that whilst Jesus, the Lamb of God, is being born of the extremely well-documented 'immaculate conception' within a lowly stable illuminated from above by the deific Star of Bethlehem, the rather less well-known Brian Cohen is entering the world several mangers up the street after having been conceived the old fashioned way. It is also perhaps worth mentioning that during the two scenes

Trivia Fact: Despite persistent rumours to the contrary, 'Jesus Christ: Lust for Glory' was only a working title and was never at any time intended for the finished movie. It was in fact Eric Idle who first came up with this title in what was meant as a throwaway comment in response to the press' seemingly never-ending quest to learn what the Python team's next movie project might be. Upon learning that Idle's remark had silenced the journalist, they too adopted the fictitious title as a 'stock response'.

where Jesus does appear, first as a baby in the manger, and later as an adult Jesus seen giving his 'Sermon on the Mount', he is treated with respect. The Pythons never had any intention of mocking Jesus Christ for, as Cleese pointed out at the time: "There's nothing about him (Jesus) that one can make fun of!"

A rep from Equity came by and said "you're keeping actors out of work, because you're playing so many different parts." We were like "what!?" That's what we do! (Terry Gilliam)

Anyway, enough of pontificating, and on with the movie, which was adapted from a script written by all six Pythons, directed by Terry Jones and produced by John Goldstone. Out of step a little from the previous Python movies, a full end-to-end script reading, simply seated round a dinner table, was recorded by the fully assembled team to see how the whole thing worked as a finished piece.

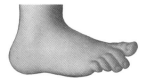

Trivia Fact: Cleese initially wanted George Lazenby, the actor best remembered for his one and only portrayal of James Bond (*On Her Majesty's Secret Service*, 1969), for the role of Jesus, as he thought it would be hilarious to have 'George Lazenby is Jesus Christ' as the movie's tagline. Whether Lazenby would have accepted is a moot point, as he was overseas working on another project at the time and therefore unavailable.

'Tis Christmas Eve, the season of good will, and against a backdrop of lilting holy music and the sound of a newborn baby's gentle cries, the gift-bearing Three Wise Men (Cleese, Chapman – who will play the adult Brian – and Palin, in numerical order) have reached the end of their journey for the Star of 'Wonder', and a Star of 'Light' has guided them to a stable within which they will gaze upon their Messiah. (Yes, I know, he's not the Messiah. He's a very naughty boy!)

Brian's mother, Mandy (Jones), however, having given birth within the last hour or so, appears somewhat agitated at the unwarranted intrusion, and is suspicious as to why three supposedly sagacious men would choose to creep around a cow shed at 2am.

"We are astrologers," says Wise Man #3 by way of explanation.

"We have come from the East," adds Wise Man #1, whose face is all but hidden beneath a mask of interlinking silver chains and baubles. When Mandy learns that the three men standing before her have come to praise and pay homage to her son, she accuses them of having followed a 'bottle' rather than some star, and tells them to clear off and praise someone else's brat. Upon hearing about the proffered gold and frankincense, whilst also discovering that myrrh was actually a very expensive ointment and not a dangerous animal that might eat her newborn baby and should therefore be drowned at the trough, she becomes all sweetness and light and even goes so far as to ask her new-found Oriental fortune-telling friends to reveal

CHAPTER SIX

her offspring's star sign. Not only does she learn that her son, whom she has decided to call 'Brian', is a 'Capricorn', but that He was also to be worshipped at all times for His being the 'Son of God' and the 'Messiah', not to mention 'King of the Jews'.

This is clearly a lot for a single Jewish mother to take in all at once, and although she's grateful for the gold and frankincense (albeit slightly less enthusiastic about the myrrh), which will enable her to supplement her low income, she makes her excuses and guides them out of the door. Within minutes, however, the Three Wise Men, having realized their error after finally coming upon the carpenter's son living three doors down, return to the Cohen residence and retrieve their gifts. Once again we hear lilting music and a newborn baby crying... but either the onset of post-natal depression, or the loss of the gifts, has taken its toll on the once-again destitute Mandy, and the apparently not-so-Messianic Brian is given something to cry about.

Trivia Fact: The main reason that George Harrison has stated that he put so much effort into funding *Life of Brian* was that it would be the only way he would be able to see another Monty Python film.

Terry Gilliam had done Jabberwocky *in the meantime, so he'd directed his own film. He hadn't really enjoyed shared direction, and then I think there was a feeling among some of the group that it would be better to have one director. And I was quite keen to do it, too. It was default, really!* (Terry Jones)

A terrific performance of someone just trying to live his life, and never playing for the obvious joke. (Michael Palin on Graham Chapman)

I think Terry instinctively understands the material, he understands what's right and wrong, what's needed and what isn't in that sense. And he works really hard, and he badgers and he just goes on. After Holy Grail, *I said, "The director's job is a dogsbody job," because we were running around doing all the work — for them, the other half of the group. It had actually started to create a kind of split in the group, because there was Terry and me over here and they were there.* (Terry Gilliam)

Many years of hardship, and relative obscurity — thirty-three to be exact — will pass before Brian sets eyes on his one-time neighbour Jesus (Kenneth Colley, perhaps best known for his role as Tony Farrell in Nicolas Roeg's 1970 film *Performance*) late one Saturday afternoon, about tea-time, when he and his mum accidentally come across his fellow Capricorn whilst making their way to a stoning. Jesus is giving his famous 'Sermon on the Mount', and judging from the large crowd already gathered, Jesus is obviously showing some promise as an up-and-coming prophet. Mrs Cohen, rather less enthralled for her hearing is not what it once was, shouts out for Jesus to "speak up!" before finally giving up altogether and suggesting that they should proceed to the stoning as planned.

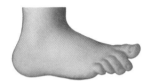

Trivia Fact: Cleese, after losing out on George Lazenby, decided to put himself forward for the role of Brian, as he believed a sustained leading role would help him to expand his range as an actor. Idle, Gilliam, Jones and Palin, however, were all in favour of Chapman taking on the role. Cleese himself soon came to realize that his old Footlights writing partner was best suited for the part, and willingly stepped aside.

Brian, however, has other ideas, for stonings in biblical times are probably a regular event, and insists on staying, which brings on an argument between mother and son, much to the consternation of those standing close by. Even Jesus is struggling to concentrate, and at this point an irate Mr Big Nose (Palin) asks for them to be quiet and is berated by his wife (Gwen Taylor) for supposedly picking the aforementioned large hooter whilst chatting to Mrs Gregory (Carol Cleveland).

Big Nose refutes his wife's allegation — and the bickering turns into a full-scale argument between the Big Noses, a Mr Cheeky (Idle) and Mr Gregory (Terence Baylor), who also complain about the noise after struggling to hear Jesus supposedly bless 'the cheesemakers', or manufacturers of any other dairy products, which is certainly food for thought. When Jesus goes on to add that the meek are going to inherit the Earth, Mrs Gregory is quite pleased that the meek will be getting something as they've been having a hell of a time of it lately. The bickering might well have ended there but Mr Cheeky is clearly enjoying himself and escalates the argument by repeatedly goading poor old Big Nose until the latter loses his rag altogether and accidentally punches Mrs Gregory, which sees Mr Gregory defending his wife's honour. Whilst Jesus' sermon is of some interest to the Cohen family, outbreaks of public disorder are obviously yesterday's news and so they instead decide to get off in time for the stoning.

As Brian and his irate mother are about to depart, he is captivated by a beautiful girl who, judging from her black garb, is a member of the

People's Front of Judea. Their leader Reg (Cleese) appears skeptical about this Jesus bloke, especially after listening to the so-called 'new kid on the block', who has offered nothing new or radical in his sermon, has seemingly pandered to anyone with a vested interest in the status quo and also, worst of all in Reg's eyes, failed completely to identify the meek as being the problem.

The 'ooh ahh' that happened over Life of Brian, *to be honest, took us all by surprise.* (Neil Innes)

I think John was quite keen to play Brian, actually, and I think others of us didn't want to do it, partly because Graham was such a good straight man, and partly because there were so many other parts, like the revolutionaries' leader, that we really wanted John to do – he wouldn't have been able to do them at the same time. The centurion had to be John, so we felt quite strongly that Graham ought to do the lead. (Terry Jones)

At last mother and son arrive at the stoning site but, as women are not permitted to attend this particular form of open-air execution, she has been forced to wear a false, and highly irritating, beard, which she may or may not have purchased from Harry the Haggler (Palin). The entrepreneurial Harry also apparently does a good line in top quality stones, including both pointed and flat varieties, and also bags of gravel for the kids. In a mix-up in one scene, a boom microphone is visible when Mrs Cohen is purchasing the stones from Harry.

"Can I have one, Mum?" asks Brian, momentarily forgetting himself, but Harry is far too occupied with the prospective sale and fails to notice Brian's faux pas.

Trivia Fact: The Who's Keith Moon was originally cast as one of the street prophets in the scene where Brian poses as a prophet in order to avoid capture by the Romans. This had come about as a result of Moon having spent a lot of time with the Python team whilst they were in the Caribbean writing the original script. Eric Idle, who would bump into Moon on the night of the drummer's untimely death, 7 September 1978, remembered that Moon had been very excited about the role. The Python team would later dedicate the movie in Moon's honour. The draft script book is actually dedicated to the legendary drummer in the early pages.

Both Brian and his bearded mother both take up a good firing position in time for the afternoon's main event: the stoning of Matthias, son of Deuteronomy of Gath (John Young) who, according to the charge being read out by the Jewish official (Cleese), has been condemned to death by stoning for having dared to suggest the lovely piece of halibut that his wife had cooked him for his supper was good enough for Jehovah.

Upon hearing the word 'Jehovah', the official again denounces Matthias as a blasphemer in an attempt to stir up the mob, but suddenly falls silent upon suspecting that there are women in attendance.

The women, all of whom are wearing false beards, shake their heads in unison, seemingly satisfying the official, who presses on with reading out the charges, but is once again interrupted from his task when Matthias is struck by a solitary stone.

"Come on, who threw that?" enquires the official, "who threw that stone?"

"She did, she did," shriek the other women, pointing towards the culprit (Idle) before realizing their mistake and quickly adopting a collective baritone, "He did, he, he, he, him, him, him, he did!"

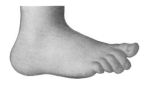

Trivia Fact: At the end of each day's filming, Chapman, who was a qualified doctor, would give on-set medical advice to the cast and crew.

Matthias uses this unexpected respite to try one last time to negate his supposed blasphemy, but this, the official warns him, has only made things worse for himself. Matthias is clearly perplexed as to what could possibly make matters worse than they already were and taunts the official by repeating the word Jehovah over and over again whilst doing a merry sand dance.

CHAPTER SIX

The official defies Matthias to say 'Jehovah' one more time, at which point he is struck by a stone for having taken the Lord's name in vain, as is the woman who threw the stone. This is all too much for the official, who insists that no one is to stone anyone until he has blown on his whistle – even if they do happen to say 'Jehovah!' Oops, too late...

The whole joke of the film is that he's not the Messiah! (Charlie Higson)

The filming of Life of Brian *was great fun, actually; it was really enjoyable. You just felt you were on a roll, you just knew it was working. But the editing wasn't much fun. I always felt with the films I'd be left out there, especially by* Brian *– everybody else would go off and do other things and I was there six, seven months later, still toiling away, trying to do the dubbing for this and that.* (Terry Jones)

Brian and his mum, having returned from the stoning, albeit the stoning of an alternate victim, are making their way back to their humble dwelling when Brian enquires if he does indeed have a 'big nose'. This has come about as a result of Mr Cheeky having earlier called Brian 'Conkface', before then enquiring if he came from 'Nose City'.

Trivia Fact: The six Pythons play forty various roles between them in the movie.

It is while Brian's mother is scolding him for always thinking about "sex", and questioning which of his appendages the girls might consider to be "too big" or "too small", that he is targeted by an ex-leper (Palin), who is on the lookout for an easy touch, or a shekel, or whichever proves easier. Upon learning from Mrs Cohen that a shekel is more money than her son earns in a month, the ex-leper offers to settle for half a shekel. When this trifling amount doesn't appear to be forthcoming, the ex-leper realises that the big-nosed individual within his sights doesn't appear to be *au fait* with the rules of 'haggling', he suggests that they cut straight to the chase and offers to settle for eighteen hundred. Just what this 'eighteen hundred' amounts to in the monetary terms of the time is anyone's guess, and this is soon rendered a moot point anyway as the ex-leper inexplicably reverts to a previous offer to settle for half a shekel.

Brian, although showing little sign of complying with the beggar's wishes is, however, intrigued by the beggar, as he'd always been led to believe that leprosy was incurable.

"Did you say 'ex-leper'?" he asks incredulously.

"That's right, sir. Sixteen years behind the bell and proud of it," replies the seemingly healed leper, before going on to explain how he had been the unsuspecting, and somewhat ungrateful, beneficiary of one of Jesus' miracles. There he was, a time-served leper with a steady trade, and the next minute some 'bloody do gooder' had robbed him of his livelihood.

Brian suggests that if the leper is so disgruntled at being cured, he should seek out Jesus and demand to be afflicted again. The leper, however, has already pondered this scenario and has decided upon asking Jesus to inflict him with a rather less- debilitating form of the disease and merely make him lame in the one leg during the middle of the week; something which will still allow him to earn a living as a beggar, but infinitely less insufferable than leprosy, which, to be blunt, is a pain in the arse. Excuse his French. The ex-leper's theoretical ramblings are cut short, however, when Mrs Cohen appears at the window and orders her son to come in and clean out his room.

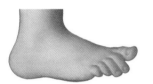

Trivia Fact: Many prominent characters in *Life of Brian*, including Mandy, Nissus Wettus and Mr Cheeky, are never named in the film, though their names can be found in the tracklisting of the soundtrack and in other places.

In a way, with Brian, we kept trying to do really dramatic things... I don't know if [that] ever works with comedy. I mean, Brian is just a more clever version of disguising the fact that they're a bunch of sketches than the others have been, because at least there's a tale that flows through the thing. But when we start setting up a thing like the chase and people are running, I don't think the audience ever gets really caught up and excited. It's jolly, it's fun and you're always slightly back from it; it's not like being in a real thriller where your guts are in your mouth. (Terry Gilliam)

As Brian (who's now a half-Denary lighter on account of the ex-leper's persistence) enters the house, he is shocked to find a 'Bloody Roman' sitting in their living room patiently waiting for fellatio. His mum attempts to assuage Brian by informing him that he should think twice before being derogatory towards the Romans, for they are not only responsible for providing a roof over their heads, but that one Roman in particular, a Centurion by the name of Naughtius Maximus, who had swept a young and impressionable Mandy Cohen off her feet with promises of a trip to Rome, a house by the Forum, her own slaves and as much gold as she could eat, was also responsible for her son's anxieties over the size of his conk.

Brian is outraged to discover that not only does his mother earn her living as a prostitute, but that he's not the 'Red Sea Pedestrian' he'd always believed himself to be, and runs off to join the P.F.J.

Brian's official induction into the People's Front of Judea... (or is it the 'Judean People's Front'? Well it can't be the 'Popular People's Front' because he's sitting thirty yards away – "splitter!")... anyway, Brian's induction comes later that afternoon at the local coliseum, where he is employed as a snack vendor selling mouth-watering tid bits such as 'lark's tongues', 'wren's livers', 'Tuscany-fried bats' and 'otter's noses'. It is during the intermission, whilst the arena is being cleared of gore, discarded body parts and the odd bit of jewellery, that he espies Reg and the other members of the revolutionary outfit, who are up in the bleachers discussing their political agenda whilst awaiting the next gladiatorial contest between Frank Goliath, the Macedonian baby-crusher (Gilliam) and Boris Mineburg (Neil Innes).

The P.F.J., as of yet, are still totally unaware of the imminent arrival of one who will shape their cause, and are listening to one of their group Judith (Sue Jones-Davies), the girl who'd caught Brian's eye earlier, making a point about how any anti-imperialist group such as theirs must reflect such a divergence of interests within its powerbase. Reg readily agrees before looking to Francis (Palin), who also agrees that Judith's point is valid, but only provided that the movement never forgets that it is the inalienable right of every man...

"Or woman," interjects Stan (Idle) who then proceeds to ensure that women are not left out of this, or any other equation involving the P.F.J., before informing his fellow anti-imperialists that he wishes to become a woman, and that they should refer to him as 'Loretta', which is his right as a man, as is the right to have babies, apparently.

When Reg informs Stan/Loretta that he can't have babies, Stan/Loretta accuses him of trying to oppress her.

Trivia Fact: *Life of Brian* **was subjected to a massive leafletting campaign led by Mary Whitehouse and others upon its release in the UK. This, of course, boosted its popularity. The leaflets alleged that the film was blasphemous, stating, among other things, that the Three Wise Men would never have been fallible enough to approach the wrong manger as they do in the beginning of the film!**

"I'm not oppressing you, Stan," replies Reg, somewhat exasperated. "You haven't got a womb. Where's the fetus going to gestate? You going to keep it in a box?"

Judith thankfully comes up with a compromise in that they agree that although Stan/Loretta can't actually have babies on account of his not having a womb, which is a simple biological fact and not the fault of the Romans, more's the pity, they can, however, agree to accept Stan/Loretta's right to have babies.

Francis readily agrees and is even willing to fight those who would oppress his brother's/sister's right to have babies, and declares that Stan/Loretta's plight is "symbolic of their struggle against oppression".

Reg, however, believes that Stan/Loretta's plight is symbolic of his struggle against reality, but he is distracted from adding further comment by Boris' apparent refusal to pit his gladiatorial skills against Frank, the aforementioned baby-crushing Macedonian. Having been forcibly ejected from the tunnel, the not-so-gladiatorial Boris discards his weapons, a trident spear and a net, and sets off circling the arena in an attempt to avoid certain death at the hands of his baby-crushing adversary. This tactic proves successful, for Frank, who is laden down with armour, suffers a cardiac arrest and keels over dead, much to the consternation of the audience.

Until we actually started, I felt, "Oh my God, what's this going to be like, so far away, filming on location in Tunisia?" Once we'd started doing it, it was great, but for example we didn't know how we were going to organise the crowds to do anything, because we couldn't communicate directly with them. (Terry Jones)

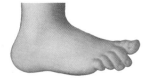

Trivia Fact: The kidnapping of Pilate's wife, in which Mrs Pilate smacks Brian on the head, was filmed but not included.

CHAPTER SIX

Brian, on account of his hating the Romans "a lot", is readily accepted into the P.F.J.'s meagre, but totally dedicated, number. His first mission as a fully-fledged, card-carrying political activist gets off to a less-than-auspicious start when he's caught red-handed (quite literally) graffiting the city walls. Fortunately for Brian, however, the Roman Centurion (Cleese) that happens upon him is far more concerned with the felon's grammatical failings, and after a brief and, in Brian's case, a somewhat painful lesson on how to correctly conjugate Latin verbs, the centurion orders Brian to write out the slogan 'Romani Ite Domum' ('Romans Go Home') 100 times before sunrise or face the prospect of having his balls cut off. (Well, education was one of the things that the Romans gave to the Judeans, right, Reg?)

Brian, although utterly exhausted, completes the task, but his balls, not to mention his neck, are once again in imminent danger of being removed when a random patrol takes a somewhat dim view of his artwork. The guards give chase but Brian is saved by Judith, who then takes him to the P.F.J.'s secret meeting house, which is owned by Matthias, whose sight is poor, and whose legs may be old and bent, but who clearly enjoys living life on the edge. The P.F.J. are formulating a plan to kidnap Pontius Pilate's wife, who will then have all her bits cut off unless Pilate agrees to "dismantle the entire apparatus of the Roman Imperialist State". (Does that include the 'aqueduct', 'sanitation', 'medicine', 'education', 'wine', 'public order', 'irrigation', 'roads', 'a fresh-water system' and 'public health' apparati?)

Trivia Fact: *Life of Brian* was re-released on 30 April 2004 in Los Angeles and New York, later moving to further US cities, as a rebuttal to Mel Gibson's *The Passion of the Christ* (as well as in honor of the film's twenty-fifth anniversary).

Upon learning that Brian is a 'doer', and has not only completed his task, but has done so 'a hundred times', and in letters 'ten-foot high', he is renamed 'Brian that is called Brian' and brought up to speed on the kidnapping plot. Whilst Dennis is providing Brian with the details, the Roman guards are seen painting the city walls to remove the graffiti.

Later that night, whilst under the cover of darkness, the P.F.J.'s highly trained commando unit enters the palace, which is situated in Caesar's Square, by way of a drain located beneath Fish Street. Their cover story, should they happen to come across any Romans, is that they are sanitation workers on their way to a conference. Reg, their glorious leader, will remain at the drain-head coordinating the assault on the account of his having a 'bad back'. (Solidarity, brothers.)

Everything appears to be going according to plan, but just as the P.F.J. commando unit is directly beneath Pilate's bedchamber they stumble

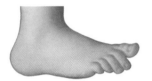

Trivia Fact: When Palin was challenging the guards by daring them to laugh, he was in fact truly daring them. The extras, although having been given strict orders by the other Pythons not to laugh, had not been given a copy of the script and had no idea what Palin was going to say or do.

upon a crack unit from a rival revolutionary group, 'Campaign for Free Galilee', who are also intent on kidnapping Mrs Pilate. Francis becomes embroiled in an argument with the C.F.F.G.'s leader, 'Deadly Dirk' (Cleese) and although Brian tries to unite the two factions against the common enemy, his pleas fall on deaf ears and the two factions slaughter each other.

Brian, upon being captured by the Roman guards who had been drawn to the sewer by all the commotion, is slung into the dungeon to await crucifixion, which is apparently the sentence prescribed for first-time offenders. This snippet of less-than-comforting information is provided by Brian's fellow 'ancient' prisoner 'Ben' (Palin), who, despite having the utmost respect for his captors, had up until the previous day been chained to the dungeon wall in an upside-down position. Ben, no doubt grateful for a spot of company, begins to berate his new cellmate for supposedly being the jailor's pet on account of the jailor (Gilliam) having spat in Brian's face, but his 'jailhouse' repartee is cut short when the centurion comes to take Brian to face the wrath, or should that be the "wwath", of the lisping Pilate.

Well, Ben was someone who's got nothing going for him at all; he's in great pain, great discomfort, but he's still incredibly aggressive. It's like the Black Knight with no legs: "Come back, you bastard, I'll kill you," or whatever he says. Ben was a bit like that, someone you just think, "Shut up, don't say anything!" But no, he's going to have a go. He's always going to have a go. He's very chirpy: He loves the Romans, the way they deal with all these things. That takes a situation where a character behaves completely opposite to how you'd expect him to behave; I suppose that's where the comedy is. (Michael Palin)

CHAPTER SIX

Bwian is thrown, or "thwown", to the floor before Pilate, who, on account of a speech impediment, weluctantly admits that the wascal spwawled before him has "spiwit", but when the Jewish wapscallion continues to pwove obstinate, Pilate orders him to be "stwuck", and vewy woughly. Bwian, who by this time has had enough of being stwuck for no apparent reason, other than his failure to understand Pilate, informs Pilate that he isn't Jewish at all, but is in fact of Roman blood.

"A Woman?"

"No, a Roman." (Slap.)

Pilate, upon hearing that Bwian's father was not only a Woman, but also a centurion in the Jerusalem garrison, enquires of his own centurion as to whether there is indeed a 'Naughtius Maximus' within the garrison.

When the centurion informs Pilate that he is convinced that there is no one of that name within the garrison, as it's a joke name such as 'Sillius Soddus', or 'Biggus Dickus', Pilate enquires as to what's so funny about the latter name for he has a vewy gweat fwiend in Wome called 'Biggus Dickus'. The mention of this naturally causes several of the guards (Guard #3, to be precise, played by Chris Langham) to start sniggering, with one unfortunate being carted off to gladiatorial school to fight wabid wild animals on account of Pilate's unwillingness to have his fwiends widdiculed by the common soldiewy. The other guards, not wishing to suffer a similar fate as their comrade, struggle to contain their mirth, but are left rolling about the fwoor upon hearing that his illustrious fwiend in Wome has a wife by the name of 'Incontinentia Buttocks'.

Terry (Jones) always says it's a heresy, and I've never understood this because a heresy is a teaching which is at variance with the Church's teaching, and I don't know in what way we're a heresy. What we are is quite clearly making fun of the way people follow religion, but not of religion itself, and the whole purpose of having that lovely scene at the start when the Three Wise Men go into the wrong stable is to say Brian is not Christ, he just gets taken for a Messiah. And that's a very important point. I will defend Life of Brian *as being a perfectly religious film.* (John Cleese)

Brian seizes his moment and scarpers, but the guards give chase and he ends up running out of both options and something solid beneath his feet as he plummets from the top of an unfinished minaret. Just

Trivia Fact: Each of the Pythons chimes in on the blasphemy topic on the commentary track of the DVD. Most interestingly, Terry Gilliam speaks of the film as 'anti-religious, anti-organized religion but not anti-spiritual' while Terry Jones explains that the initial protests over the film weren't led by Christian organizations, but rather the Rabbinical Association of New York, who were infuriated by the costume that John Cleese wears in the stoning scene!

as he is about to be splattered on the dusty gravel below, however, he is plucked from the sky by an alien spaceship, manned by two very bizarre-looking, Cyclops-like creatures that wouldn't have been out of place in *Star Wars,* which, incidentally, was filmed just a few miles further along into the desert. The ship, fuelled by Gilliam's well-documented left-of-centre imagination, soars off into the stratosphere with a course set for planet Rozak Kaibak, but God has obviously decided that Brian's work on earth is not yet finished and sends another alien craft to intervene. The unidentified aliens open fire and score a direct hit, sending the Cyclopean craft and Brian plummeting back to earth where it crashes less than a stone's throw from the unfinished minaret and his Roman pursuers.

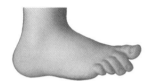

Trivia Fact: John Cleese can be heard in the commentary track of the Criterion edition of *Life of Brian* referring to Jesus as 'really rather a good guy'!

Exploding spaceships must have been a common sight in Judea because the guards pay this one no heed whatsoever as they rush past, nor do they appear unduly concerned over the fact that Brian, a fellow mortal, has emerged from the burning craft without so much as a scratch.

Brian, realising that the Romans aren't about to give up their chase any time soon, seeks to deceive his pursuers by adopting a cunning disguise and purchases a false beard, which he claims is for his mother. But guess who's selling the beards? That's right, Harry the Haggler, who refuses to part with the beard, which is of the highest quality, and "not of the goat", without first engaging in a spot of haggling. His dying grandmother would probably be turning on her deathbed if she thought her Harry was one to put profit before a good haggle.

After a lesson on how to haggle, Brian comes away with the aforementioned beard, which he bought for sixteen shekels, and

also a four-shekel gourd, which was apparently worth ten. But let's not go there.

Meanwhile, back at Matthias' house, Reg is trying to restore confidence in the now-seriously depleted P.F.J. by insisting that there is no need for them to be down-hearted over one total catastrophe, and puts forward the motion for their seven fallen comrades to be entered into the minutes as probationary martyrs.

In a continuity error, Francis (Palin) is killed during the P.F.J. commando unit's fight with the 'C.F.F.G.' in the sewer beneath Pilate's palace, yet is present at the subsequent meeting. (And if he wasn't killed during the fight then why wasn't he captured and thrown into the dungeon with Brian?)

One might have expected Reg and the others to be delighted that one of the martyrdoms could be put on hold, and they probably would have been had it not been for Brian having, albeit inadvertently, led the Fifth Legion to their headquarters. Matthias buys the P.F.J. precious time to seek out hiding places while he runs through his catalogue of ailing infirmities, but the centurion is having none of it and orders his men to search the interior. The soldiers march in at the double, accompanied by ridiculously overdubbed stomping boots and clanging metal that makes a routine house search sound like the German Sixth Army's advance on Stalingrad. While the soldiers are conducting their farcical search for Brian, who is far more concerned with the sturdiness of the rickety wooden conservatory that is serving as a hiding place, the centurion enquires as to whether Matthias is aware that the penalty for harbouring known criminals is crucifixion. Matthias, however, remains unimpressed (well, he was very blasé about the prospect of being stoned to death), and informs the centurion that there are worse ways to die, such as being stabbed – and crucifixion isn't a bad way to go, as it at least gets you out in the open air.

Trivia Fact: In addition to five deleted scenes and other special features, the Criterion edition of *Life of Brian* includes four British radio spots for the film. Each of the ads feature the voices of people claiming to be the mothers of various of the Pythons (as well as one person purporting to be Michael Palin's dentist) and recommending the film for various off-kilter reasons.

The danger has supposedly passed, but just as Reg is berating Brian for his stupidity they are forced into hiding once again, as the Fifth Legion has apparently left one stone unturned. The stone is suitably turned but yields nothing more subversive than a wooden spoon. The Romans depart for a second time, with wooden spoon in tow, but return within seconds, which, as Matthias readily points out, is hardly fair as the P.F.J. haven't even had time to hide again. This matters little, however, for Brian's weight has proved too much for his rickety sanctuary, and he plummets to the ground, but manages to break his fall, not to mention the neck of the unsuspecting prophet upon whom he has landed.

Brian, although once again grateful to find himself still in one piece, is forced to assume the recently deposed prophet's mantle, but as he hasn't done much prophesying he seeks inspiration from the other prophets. These include the 'Blood and Thunder' Prophet (Gilliam), the False Prophet (Charles McKeown) and the Boring Prophet (Palin).

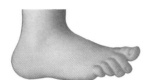

Trivia Fact: The most interesting of the cut scenes in the Criterion edition of *Life of Brian* is one which provides background and some explanation for the Judean People's Front's 'crack suicide squad' which comes to rescue Brian at the end of the film before committing mass suicide.

Old Blood and Thunder certainly stands out from his fellow prophets as he has the appearance of a half-crazed aboriginal, and looks most impressive dressed in an eye-catching red and black ensemble, which is set off by a wooden staff with two human hands, mounted upon it. His topic of the day is the 'Bezan', which is apparently 'large' and 'black', with eyes the colour of blood, and also how the Whore of Babylon shall ride forth across the land on a three-headed serpent, which will result in a 'great rubbing of parts'. The False Prophet speaks of a demon brandishing a nine-bladed sword. Nine-bladed! Not two, or five, or seven, but a nine-bladed sword, which will be wielded upon all wretched sinners. (The False Prophet's gruff Irish accent cannot help but draw comparisons to the often extreme Northern Irish politician and religious leader Reverend Ian Paisley.)

The Boring Prophet, however, is, of little use, for he is rambling on about rumours of things 'going astray', little things possessed of a 'raffia-worked base' that comes with an attachment. And of how the young shall not know where these things lieth, even though their fathers had apparently put them down only the night before... ZZZzzzzzzz.

Brian is also drawing attention to himself, but only because he isn't actually saying anything, which, it has to be said, is most unusual for a prophet – especially one that has an (albeit tiny) audience; even the Roman sentry standing directly beneath Brian's feet is becoming suspicious. It's time to shit or get off the pot, and poor old Brian appears to be verbally constipated – but then he remembers snippets from Jesus' Sermon on the Mount, and calls for his fellow men not to pass judgment on each other unless they are also willing to be judged. He's on a bit of a roll now, but keeps being pestered by Dennis (not the seemingly immortal Dennis of the P.F.J., but another Dennis, played by Terence Baylor) who has his eyes on Brian's gourd.

As Brian has no need for the gourd, he readily gives it away, but Dennis, like Harry, cannot allow a transaction to pass without first engaging in a bit of haggling. Brian, however, has neither the time nor the inclination to haggle, and as the Roman guards are slowly making their way in, he calls upon his audience to consider the lilies in the field. When this fails to elicit much of a response he swiftly moves on to the birds, for if the birds don't have jobs yet are doing alright, then why should they, the people, who are more important than the birds, have need to worry?

Such radical thinking, like the unemployed birds, goes completely over the audience's collective head, so Brian decides to explain his message by way of a parable which told of Simon and Adrian, two brothers born into servitude who, in later life, are given talents by their master. Brian really should have paid more attention in parable class for the audience has totally lost interest, not to mention the plot, and are moving on to the next prophet. Brian might not care were it not for the fact that the Romans are now heading straight towards him, and in his panic he blurts out the first thing that comes into his head, which has something to do with the 'blessed' coveting their neighbour's ox, and inhibiting their girth, but not only that they shall be given...

And it is here that Brian, were he interested in taking up a career in prophesising, might have learned the valuable lesson that the best way to keep an audience is to always leave them wanting more, but Brian isn't, and has nothing on his mind except going home to his mum. The audience, however, which is growing by the minute, has other ideas, for they are still in need of an answer, so much so in fact, that not even a blind beggar is allowed to get in the way. When it is rumoured that Brian possesses the secret of eternal life, his status is quickly elevated to that of 'Master' and a new religion is born when one of his new disciples (Cleveland) grabs His gourd from Dennis' grasp – despite it still being under offer.

Trivia Fact: The man who falls to the ground and says 'let us pray' when the crazed mob is following Brian is Spike Milligan in another cameo.

Brian, who's obviously getting good at giving people the slip by now, takes advantage of the commotion to make another getaway, and his followers assume that His disappearance is due to Him having ascended up into the celestial heavens. Their ecstasy at witnessing this wondrous miracle is dampened, but only slightly, when Brian is spotted ducking into a back alley.

Brian flees the city and heads up into the surrounding hills in the hope that the mob, faced with the prospect of a gruelling mid-afternoon run, will lose their fervour and give up the chase. But he obviously hasn't taken into account just what having a new Messiah to follow means to the local populace. It means so much, in fact, that when they come upon the sandal that Brian had been forced to abandon in his bid to escape, a certain number of His followers see it as another sign, and yes, another religion is born, or perhaps we should make that a multitude of fledgling religions, for the crowd quickly subdivides into several splinter factions with one faction following His example by removing one shoe and holding it aloft, while another faction insists that His message is to go forth and gather all the shoes. The newly formed 'Gourdenes', however, dismiss the sandal and are still for following the gourd, which is now no ordinary gourd, but the 'Holy Gourd of Jerusalem', while another faction believes that, like 'Him', they should not think of things of the body, but of the head and the face.

A prophet by the righteous name of 'Spike' (Milligan) looks on in bemusement as the differing factions begin arguing amongst themselves as to which of them is the one true religion, and calls upon everyone to pray in unison to 'Him that has cometh to them like the seed of the grain', but his words fall upon deaf ears, for by this time the crowd has long departed to continue its search for the Master.

Brian, although having had a good head start on the fanatical crowd, is now hopelessly lost, but just when all appears to be lost he happens upon a ditch which is home to the bearded, naked and supposedly holy Simon (Jones). Brian beseeches the holy hermit to give him directions back down to the river, but Simon, unbeknownst to Brian, has taken the vow of silence, a vow that he has kept for eighteen years, and therefore cannot answer. Brian is also desperate for the quiet life and leaps down into the ditch, but the eighteen-year-long silence is shattered, along with Simon's toe, and the hermit's cries bring the crowd running.

One of the shoe followers, Arthur (Cleese), who's an old hand at following Messiahs, informs Brian that his people, having walked for miles, are weary and in need of food, but that there is no food to be had in the mountains. When Brian, not having fish paste sandwiches or a bottle of claret to hand, points to the clump of juniper bushes several yards away, his followers immediately proclaim it a miracle. Simon, knowing that his survival depends on those precious perennial berries, has no intention of sharing them with a bunch of deluded 'townies', and vaults out of his ditch determined to defend his lunch.

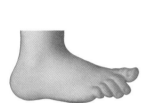

Trivia Fact: One of the movie's more testing moments came during Chapman's nude scene when a stark-bollock naked Brian throws back the shutters of his room and discovers hordes of disciples waiting outside – the problem being that half of the three hundred or so extras were women, and Muslim women to boot, whose strict laws forbade them to gaze upon a naked penis, and a gay Englishman's penis to boot.

Trivia Fact: *Life of Brian* was originally to be financed by EMI (for £2m), but the corporation announced it was reneging on the deal after Lord Delfont, EMI's sixty-nine year-old Chief Executive, finally got around to reading the script.

CHAPTER SIX

Arthur and the others, however, have momentarily lost their appetite, for the crazy hermit has suddenly regained the ability to speak after eighteen years, clearly another miracle and cause for praise. The crowd beseeches Brian to stamp on their feet so that they may have their afflictions and ailments cured.

After witnessing a supposedly cured blind man tumble headlong into the ditch, Brian implores the crowd to believe him when he says that he isn't the Messiah, but in doing so he inadvertently confirms his deific status, for only the true Messiah would try to deny his divinity. Brian, realizing the hopelessness of his situation, gives up and proclaims himself to be the Messiah before issuing his first divine instruction in that his flock should 'fuck off' in no uncertain terms. Simon, however, has no intention of fucking off, and begins to berate Brian for having first broken his foot, which had in turn caused him to break his vow of silence, not to mention offering his dinner to all and sundry. But his verbal assault on the Chosen One is decried as heresy, and he is carried away by the frenzied mob to lose a lot more than his juniper berries.

Trivia Fact: As Christmas approached, the movie's distributors (CIC), trying to avoid stirring up even more problems, elected to launch *Life of Brian* in just one London cinema, and wait until after the religiously-sensitive period was over before putting the movie out on general release. On 8 November 1979, against a backdrop of carol-singing protesters gathered outside, the movie was shown at the Plaza, situated on Lower Regent Street. It went on to break box-office records, taking in £40,000 in its first week, smashing the cinema's previous house record, set four years earlier by Steven Spielberg's *Jaws*.

Brian tries to intervene on Simon's behalf, but soon loses interest, subsequently followed by his 'cherry', thanks to having spent the night wrapped within the arms of the lovely Judith. Brian's dream of spending the rest of his life with Judith at his side is cruelly shattered when he pushes back the shutters of his bedroom window to find a milling throng of early morning worshippers, many of whom are holding staffs with either gourds or sandals attached in a show of affiliation, awaiting the arrival of their Messiah.

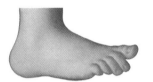

Trivia Fact: George Harrison appears yet again in the crowd of followers that Brian is confronted with after spending the night with Judith. He's the man with the Liverpool accent and full beard who says 'ello'.

When Mrs Cohen awakes, she is none-too-pleased about the large 'multitude' gathered outside her front door, and immediately suspects (as only a mother can) that her son is somehow responsible. Now she already knows that her son isn't a Messiah (the Three Wise Men having put paid to that idea some thirty-three years earlier) and goes to the window to enlighten the crowd of this fact. She's also none too keen on Brian having dared to bring some 'Welsh tart' home with him, and after finally managing to tear her eyes away from Judith's 'Garden of Eden' she sends Brian to the window so that he can disperse the crowd, only for her to end up engaging the crowd in a spot of pantomime repartee. At first she appears to be softening on account of the crowd hailing her as being 'Blessed' and calling her 'Hosanna', but she soon takes affront at being asked if she was a 'virgin'. (Well, the crowd did warn her that it was a personal question... and if only they knew that her scrapped knees did not come from scrubbing the floors).

Brian is coerced into going down for a 'meet and greet' session with his followers, which perhaps is not the wisest decision he's ever made, given the fact that he's still a wanted man. Arthur, who seems to have elected himself as the new Messiah's right-hand man, introduces Brian to Mr Papadopolous (George Harrison) who has agreed to allow Brian the use of his 'Mount' on Sundays, before then setting about sorting the crowd into various queues depending on their ailments. Those possessed by devils are ordered to be quiet, the incurables are told to wait their turn, while the women taken in sin are lined up against the wall (facing which way?). And although Arthur is proving himself most able in protecting Brian from having sick babies pushed in front of His face or unwarranted intrusions from the likes of Mr Gregory, whose wife is apparently in need of a cure for her headache, he is powerless to prevent Brian from being 'nicked' by the dogged centurion who, like the Mountie (apart from when taking time out to sing the chorus line from the 'Lumberjack Song'), always gets his man.

I was just totally indignant at the level of debate. I think I'd expected there to be an argument, I'd expected there to be opposition, but the level of it was so depressing. It was just, "They're comedy writers, therefore nothing they say is to be taken seriously. They have no serious point to make." I mean, John and I went on television with a bishop and prominent religious writer, and they were pathetic – they were just sort of sneering at us for attempting to deal with this subject. And the rest of it was just laughable because people were saying it was Python's send-up of Jesus. No, he isn't Jesus, he's this character. (Michael Palin)

Brian is once again brought before Pilate who, although willing to admit that Bwian has given them (the Romans) a good wun for their money, guawantees that there will be no chance of Bwian wepeating his eawier escapades and orders him to be sent for cwucifixion. The centurion is more than happy to comply, but enquires if he might first be allowed to disperse the crowd gathered in the street below. Pilate is most taken aback by this as today is the feast of Passover and he hasn't addwessed the cwowd yet, which was obviously the centurion's intention. To make matters worse, Pilate has invited his good friend Biggus Dickus (Chapman) up from Rome to hear him speak.

Trivia Fact: Some of the scenes in *Life of Brian* were filmed in the leftover sets from Franco Zeffirelli's 1977 miniseries *Jesus of Nazareth*.

"Weally, Centuwion," says Pilate, "I'm suwpwised to hear a man like you being wattled by a wabble of wowdy webels."

"A... bit thundery, sir," replies the bewildered centurion.

Meanwhile, back at P.F.J. HQ, Reg and his fellow subversives are drawing up a five-year plan which should see them attain world supremacy, but only if they can manage to get off their collective arse

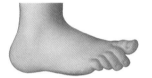

Trivia Fact: An early idea for the movie involved a scene where Jesus, a skilled carpenter, is frustrated at being crucified upon a poorly constructed cross.

and smash the Roman Empire within the first twelve months. A call for action and not words is greeted with much chest-pounding, for they are all agreed that no amount of sitting around talking, passing resolutions and making clever speeches will shift a single Roman soldier from their homeland. So what do they do upon learning from a distraught Judith that Brian has been dragged away for crucifixion? They decide to hold a discussion on a new motion, but not until they've held a ballot, because no self-respecting political activist can possibly act on a resolution without first having voted on the aforementioned resolution...

Judith is beside herself, and not simply because Brian has proved himself to be amazing both in and out of the bed sheets, and demands action that day, but Reg is not one to put his head in the lion's mouth without first having decided upon a motion, which will first require a resolution... not to mention a vote...

The film has appealed to many seriously religious people, including the Dalai Lama and some Jesuits. It also plays better in Catholic countries – go figure! But it was wonderful – anger is the hallmark of the closed mind, and we certainly flushed out some raving bigots, and that was part of the joy of it. (Eric Idle)

Brian is lined up (on the left) with the other unfortunates selected for the Romans' 'Thanksgiving Special Crucifixion', and finds himself reunited with Mr Cheeky, who lives up to his name by conning the Roman in charge of crucifixion duty, Nissus Wettus (Palin), ably assisted by the mentally-challenged jailor (Gilliam), and his stuttering assistant (Idle), into believing that he hasn't actually done anything wrong and is therefore to be free so that he can go off and live on an island somewhere (preferably one that isn't subjugated to Roman rule). The gullible Nissus readily accepts Mr Cheeky's tale and is about to order his release, but instead of going off to book a one-way ticket to the land of anywhere-but-here, the leg-pulling Judean confesses to his attempted deception and goes through the door to take up his cross.

All is not lost for Brian, however, for it is customary on such special occasions for Wome to pwove its fwiendship by weleasing a wongdoer from its pwisons. The Judeans gathered below certainly take the Passover out of Pilate by requesting that the Roman Procurator of Judea should welease 'Woger', or maybe even 'Wodewick', who's not only a wobber and a wapist, he's also a pickpocket.

The centurion comes to Pilate's rescue by suggesting that there are prisoners worthy of amnesty such as 'Samson the Sadducee Strangler', or 'Silas the Syrian Assassin', or even the 'several seditious scribes from Caesarea'. This tactful ploy might have worked had it not been for the fact that Biggus Dickus – who not only leads a cwack legion, but also wanks very highly in Wome – just happens to suffer from a terrible lisp. His inthithtence to address, or should that be "addreth" the crowd, and his offer to release "Thamson the Thadducee Thtrangler", soon has the Judeans rolling around in hysterics.

Meanwhile, Brian is trying desperately to hold up proceedings by enquiring if he might be allowed to see a lawyer. Nissus, although sympathetic as he believes 140 crucifixions – Passover or no Passover – to be such a waste of human life, has, however, still got his orders and a quota to fulfil, and has no alternative but to send Brian through with the others. Once the crucifixion party has been taken through the list of pre-judicial murder instructions, which include maintaining a good straight line, keeping to a steady pace with three lengths between each man, and a timely reminder to keep the back hard up against the crossbeam, the condemned are led away to Crucifixion Mount, which is but a ten-minute walk from the city's

Trivia Fact: The crucifixion scene was recorded in freezing temperatures in the morning, which is why John Cleese can be seen wearing clothes, unlike the other actors. He couldn't take the cold.

walls and provides something of interest for the sentries to watch during what would otherwise be a very monotonous shift.

As they are being led through the streets to serve as a warning to their fellow Judeans that crime, or insurgency against the Roman Empire, does not pay, a saintly passerby (Jones) offers to assist one of the condemned in shouldering such a heavy burden. The condemned man, perhaps none-too-surprisingly given the circumstances, readily offloads the heavy cross onto the kindly, yet foolish, Samaritan, and scarpers into the crowd.

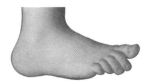

Trivia Fact: The credits of *Life of Brian* include a mention for 'Moose Choreography'!

Brian's only hope of salvation now lies with Judith, who at that precise moment is pushing her way through the crowd gathered outside Pilate's palace. When Pilate offers to give the crowd one last chance to have a prisoner released, just so long as it isn't a "Wueben", a "Weginald", a "Wudolph the Wed-Nosed Waindeer" or a "Thpenther Trathy", she readily shouts out calling for Brian to be weleased, I mean released. The wily Pilate initially suspects that this is just another ploy for the crowd to mock him, but upon discovering that they do have a Brian, regardless of the fact that he has just been sent for crucifixion, he weadily agwees to welease the aforementioned Bwian of Nazaweth and orders the centurion to see to the wel... release.

The centurion arrives at the jail but he's too late, although he does learn that they, the jailor and his assistant, apparently have "lumps of it 'round the back". How either Gilliam or Idle managed to keep a straight face whilst playing these roles is a testament to their insanity, and they are responsible for one of the movie's funniest moments when, having been left alone once again, the pair shed their mental and speech deficiencies to conduct a normal conversation.

It was quite bracing at the time; also it had a delightfully Pythonic effect, in that in this country the film was passed by the British Board of Film Censors, but local councils could ban it under a rather obscure law governing hygiene in cinemas! For some reason, under this law, they could decide not to show a certain film, and a number of councils decided not to show Life of Brian. (Michael Palin)

As Brian is fastened to his cross, he can at least take some consolation that he will be spending his last remaining hours on earth, which may be quite a few given the fact that his and all the other crucifixes have been fitted with footrests, amongst, well, if not exactly friends, then certainly acquaintances who will be able to keep him company – acquaintances like Mr Big Nose and Mr and

Mrs Gregory, who are bemoaning their lot about non-Jews having been crucified in the Jewish section, and there's also Mr Cheeky, who appears very nonchalant about the whole crucifixion thingy, but then again this could be because he's expecting to be rescued in a day or two – that's if his randy brother, who's apparently up and down like the Assyrian Empire, can keep off the 'tail' for more than twenty minutes.

In another error, as the camera pans along the row of crosses during the crucifixion scene, a man wearing a suit and tie can be seen walking in the background.

Brian's spirits soar like the one-eyed aliens' spaceship when Reg and the other members of the P.F.J. arrive, but alas for Brian, they have come not to rescue him but rather to convey their sincere brotherly and sisterly greetings. Reg then goes on to inform Brian that not only will his death stand as a landmark in the continued struggle to liberate the parentland from the Roman Imperialist aggressors, excluding those involved with providing Judea with all the comforts of Rome, and also those Romans contributing to the welfare of Jews of both sexes and hermaphrodites, but also adds, on a personal note, his admiration for what Brian is doing for the cause at what must be, for himself at least, a very trying time. As a final tribute, he and the other members of the P.F.J. proceed to sing a rousing verse of 'He's a Jolly Good Fellow', but Brian is feeling anything but jolly and is so preoccupied with cursing his one-time fellow revolutionaries that he fails to notice the arrival of the centurion or hear his name being called out.

Mr Cheeky, on the other hand, knows a Roman bearing free pardons when he sees one and wastes little time in informing the centurion that he is in

Trivia Fact: During the final crucifixion scene, a man can be seen walking in the background wearing a suit and tie!

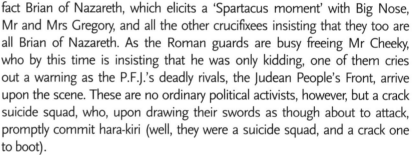

fact Brian of Nazareth, which elicits a 'Spartacus moment' with Big Nose, Mr and Mrs Gregory, and all the other crucifixees insisting that they too are all Brian of Nazareth. As the Roman guards are busy freeing Mr Cheeky, who by this time is insisting that he was only kidding, one of them cries out a warning as the P.F.J.'s deadly rivals, the Judean People's Front, arrive upon the scene. These are no ordinary political activists, however, but a crack suicide squad, who, upon drawing their swords as though about to attack, promptly commit hara-kiri (well, they were a suicide squad, and a crack one to boot).

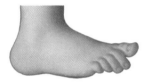

Trivia Fact: The version of 'Always Look on the Bright Side of Life' that appears in the film was recorded by Eric Idle in a hotel room, with mattresses leaned up against the walls.

Next on the scene are the two women in Brian's life, and although neither one has come to rescue him, Judith does at least offer some consolation in that she now finally understands, thanks to Reg's explanation, what it is that he is doing and that she will (sniff) never forget him. Mr Frisbee III (Idle), who's one cross behind and to Brian's right, offers encouragement to Brian in that he should cheer up and, when he's chewing on life's gristle, he shouldn't grumble but give a little whistle and then things might just turn out for the best, and (queue music)... to "always look on the bright side of life..."

In the end, we'd been through all the possible dangers of people dismissing it and I think we'd come out with something intellectually defensible, so I quite enjoyed the reaction. Because in many ways it made us exactly what Python is about really, the reaction from the sort of people who were the inspiration for Python: the little petty local officials who close cinemas for hygiene because they don't like the comedy film about the Bible story. In a way, comedy doesn't want to change the world, and it never does, but occasionally you need to have your own prejudices reinforced! These people still exist, so there's a reason to be doing Python! (Michael Palin)

CHAPTER SEVEN:
THE MEANING OF LIFE

Why are we here? What's life all about?
Is God really real? Or is there some doubt?
Well, tonight, we're going to sort it out,
For, tonight, it's The Meaning of Life.

The Meaning of Life was the fourth, and last, movie from the Monty Python team, and although it is fair to say that it fails to live up to the comedic standards of *Holy Grail* or *Life of Brian*, it is, however, still a very entertaining movie. Of the team members, Eric Idle still thinks the film is vastly underrated. The two-disc DVD, which was released in 2003, is a particular must for all Python aficionados, as it features a cornucopia of delightful and amusing extras, including 'Snipped Bits', which includes several deleted scenes that didn't make it to the final cut. Our particular favourite of these is the 'Martin Luther' sketch, and even Terry Jones, who himself portrayed the Sixteenth Century German leader of the Protestant Reformation with an apparent obsession for spoons – especially voluptuous virginal ones – admits in the accompanying voiceover, that the decision to cut this sketch was one of the more difficult choices that he'd had to make whilst attempting to edit the finished movie. There is also a 'Making of' documentary in which the five surviving Pythons talk candidly about the movie's merits and also its shortcomings. Jones (who co-directed the movie), Palin and Gilliam take a philosophical approach in that although *Meaning of Life* may have suffered as a result of the team having perhaps been a bit hasty in rushing to make another movie so soon after completing *Life of Brian*, they are pleased with the finished product nevertheless.

Not hard. John was the one who was reluctant; we simply started writing without him. But we found it hard to find a theme, even when he came aboard. (Eric Idle)

Idle is equally pleased with their collective efforts, but in hindsight wishes that he and the rest of the team had taken a step back and waited for a couple of weeks before getting together again to pour over the script, as this may have resulted in them singling out one particular character, i.e., the young schoolboy Biggs, who is seen in later life as a captain during WWI, and would have given the proposed movie a more centralized theme. They could then have omitted the captions that served to highlight the movie's sketch nature.

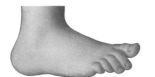

Trivia Fact: In order to persuade Universal Studios to make the film, the Pythons wrote a poem about the script, budget and content of the film. The poem being recited by Eric Idle was featured as the introduction to the film on the special edition DVD.

– From Wikipedia.com

This opportunity was missed, however, partly due to Cleese's other work commitments, but also because of his reluctance to spend, or waste, any more of his time on the project, which he likens to a 'ragbag of sketches'. This is a rather strange admission given that sketches are most definitely of his 'idiom'. It is well documented that whilst the team were ensconced in the Caribbean to work on the script they suffered from a temporary bout of 'writer's block', which was the main reason behind their decision to book a series of live shows at the Hollywood Bowl in Los Angeles, and indeed if, as Cleese claims in the documentary, he'd have had his way, the project would have been abandoned in favour of spending the remaining ten days on vacation.

That was the trouble really, it was getting increasingly hard to get together, and it showed, I think. We'd meet and we'd read out our material, then we wouldn't meet again for another two months or something, and then we'd get together again, have another read out of

material, and it seemed to be getting nowhere. I think we spent about a year doing that, meeting on and off and getting this pile of stuff together. (Terry Jones)

Thankfully, the others were somewhat reluctant to throw in the towel, or even to drape it over a sun lounger, which may have had something to do with the fact that Universal Studios had given them a $10,000,000 budget, and the clock was ticking. This in itself is somewhat amazing – not that the clock was ticking, but that the Pythons had been given a shed-load of cash when they as yet didn't have a script. There was, however, method in Universal's madness, for on the strength of having landed the Pythons the studio was able to attract to its roster a whole host of top comedians, including Eddie Murphy, who they'd been after for years.

According to Gilliam, an early idea was to base the movie's theme on a futuristic WWIII with armies going into battle wearing sponsorships and advertising logos on their uniforms, which would not only be highly amusing but would also be equally innovative in terms of financing the movie. This idea sadly came to naught, but once the team did get down to some serious writing, which could be construed as a contradiction in terms, it began to emerge that the proposed movie was going to be a series of sketches loosely based on the seven stages of man. Cleese, however, was initially against the idea of sketches, as he believed that such a movie could only realistically be expected to hold the viewers' attention for around forty minutes. Once again Cleese appears to have either been overruled, or willing to relent to the Pythons' collective will, which was proved correct as the movie went on to win an award at that year's Cannes Film Festival. Up until that point the Pythons' celluloid offerings had merited one BAFTA nomination, and even that was for the costume design on *Life of Brian*, so to discover that *Meaning of Life* had been named as Britain's official entry at Cannes left the six Pythons utterly bemused and bewildered, especially Chapman, as the movie was in neither French or Russian, nor was it particularly 'arty' – but then again, this would provide opportunities for more sex.

I always said, "Let's do a sketch film, I'm sure we could do a sketch film and make it work", just to show we can. Because there was this feeling maybe a sketch film you couldn't sustain for more than an hour. And because we'd never done a sketch film – And Now for Something Completely Different I never really counted because I thought it was a bit half-arsed, it wasn't conceived as a film really. (Terry Jones)

Trivia Fact: Eric's one-sheet proposal for the movie contained the following short poem... "There's everything in this movie, everything that fits, from the Meaning of Life in the Universe, to girls with great big tits!"

We never found the theme till the end. I think it would have been perfect if we had given it one extra draft and it had become the Seven Ages of Man as well, with the story of one person, growing up at various ages through time. We nearly got there, but again John was reluctant to meet, so we just went ahead and shot it anyway. It still has great stuff in it and is still marvellously offensive! (Eric Idle)

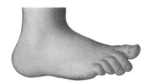

Trivia Fact: In 2002, a French comedy troupe dubbed 'Les Pythons' opened a French version of Monty Python at the Palais des Glaces in Paris, translating and re-interpreting twenty-five sketches and songs for a French audience. Terry Gilliam gave the show a glowing review.

Legend has it that when Jones and co-director Ian MacNaughton arrived in Cannes, they jokingly informed the waiting journalists that the Pythons had bribed the judges to secure first place, which saw them splattered across the front pages of the following day's local newspapers. The joke backfired, however, when the movie actually won. When Jones and MacNaughton went up on stage to receive the award, Jones further fuelled the conspiratorial flames by jokingly informing the judges that their bribe money was stashed under the sink in the gents' toilets.

Idle believes that they owed their success at Cannes to the team's decision to remove Gilliam's 'Crimson Permanent Assurance' sketch from the main movie, and instead edit it down to a more judicious sixteen minutes in order to present it to the Cannes cognoscenti as a featurette. The decision was made on the grounds that the segment, which when finished lasted some twenty-five minutes, was way too long to be included in the main movie as there was no way that they could possibly follow on from there with another sketch, and it would also inevitably slow the movie down. The original idea was for the 'Crimson Permanent Assurance' segment to be an animation piece, but as Gilliam had just spent the last couple of years making two animated films, he was loathe to embark on another, and instead elected to create a cinematic epic. The American, much to the belated envy of his fellow Pythons, was not only given free reign and left to his own devices, he was even provided with his own soundstage, cast and crew. He often jokingly cites his reason for going over budget on the project as "no one told me to stop".

And so, without further ado, Monty Python proudly presents...

'The Crimson Permanent Assurance'
(Or 'Full Speed Ahead, Mr Cohen!')

In the bleak days of Nineteen Hundred and Eighty Three, as England languishes in the doldrums of a ruinous monetarist policy, the good and loyal men of the Permanent Assurance Company, a once-proud family firm, recently fallen on hard times, are straining against the yoke of their oppressive new corporate management. How much longer can these loyal and dedicated men be expected to maintain a dignified silence while being treated as though they are little more than Second Century galley slaves?

Pushed beyond the bounds of decent and reasonable victimization, the aged retainers take their destiny into their own hands and... mutiny!

The order is given to break open the weapons, which comprise of homemade cutlasses with razor-sharp extractor blades, and any other general office equipment that might do a man some damage. The yuppie young-bloods may be *au fait* on all the latest computer techniques, and brimming with business acumen, but they have no stomach for a good old-fashioned set-to, and are soon overwhelmed. Once the building is secure, the order is given for the men to get out into the rigging, which is the scaffolding used by the workers from Acme Stone Cleaning, and to then unfurl the sails, which are little more than Acme's protective dust sheets. Yet where there is a will, there are anchors aweigh: The giant monolith breaks free of its moorings, and Crimson Permanent Assurance is launched upon the high seas of international finance.

Trivia Fact: The building used in the featurette is actually the Lloyd's of London maritime insurance building.

Up, up, up your premium,
Up, up, up your premium,
Scribble away...

The elderly retainers-turned-pirates, having cast off the starched vestiges of their former lives, set their sights on the richest jewel in I.M.F.'s crown, a financial district (which is not too dissimilar in

appearance from New York's Wall Street), swollen with multinationals, conglomerates and fat, bloated merchant banks.

Hidden behind the faceless, towering canyons of glass, the world of high finance sits smug and self-satisfied, as their future, in the shape of their past, slips silently through the streets, returning to wreak a terrible revenge. Adopting, adapting and improving traditional business practices, the men of Permanent Assurance put into motion an audacious, and totally unsuspected, takeover bid by unleashing a ferocious broadside of filing cabinet drawers that shatter the silence, not to mention their nemesis' glass edifice, and almost decapitate the hapless cleaners from Stephens & Carter (Palin and Gilliam).

Whilst the corporate fat cats are reeling from the devastating broadside, which has sent their precious balance sheets and print outs billowing around the office, the Permanent Assurance building moves up alongside and the retainers, with grappling coat racks at the ready, prepared to board. The hand-to-hand fighting is bloody, but victory is assured when the conglomerate's computer is destroyed by a telling poke from the pointed end of an umbrella, and the conglomerate's chief executive, knowing that no quarterly dividend can be expected, throws himself out of the window and plummets to his death.

We originally thought he was doing a five-minute animation ('Crimson Permanent Assurance'); it was only when we heard Terry wanted another million dollars or whatever it was, we suddenly realised it was a whole different feature going on! We kept going to his studio next door, and he had these huge sets compared to what we had. (Terry Jones)

But what was interesting afterwards, when we started cutting it down, it just wouldn't stay in the film. And I cut it shorter and shorter, and the others kept saying, "No, it's still too long." The rhythms of it are just totally different rhythms than Python rhythms, it's not like that – it's very long! (Terry Gilliam)

And so, heartened by their initial success, the desperate, and reasonably violent, men of Permanent Assurance battle on until, as the sun slowly sets in the west, the outstanding return on their bold business venture becomes apparent: The once-proud financial giants lay in ruins, their assets stripped and their policies in tatters.

And so the men of Crimson Permanent Assurance sail off into the ledgers of history. One by one, the financial capitals of the world

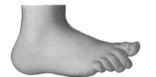

Trivia Fact: The chief executive is played by Matt Frewer, who achieved lasting fame as the futuristic TV presenter Max Headroom.

Trivia Fact: The movie's original title was 'Monty Python's Fish Film'.

Trivia Fact: The names of the companies that are owned by the 'Prize' and listed on the boardroom wall are a repeating list of puns and in-jokes from later scenes in the movie, such as: 'Rubber Goods, Inc.', 'Liver Donors, Inc.', 'Huge Horace Mann & Yore, Ltd.', 'X Tortion World Wide', 'R. J. McArthur Parks' and 'O. Verpaid Associates, Ltd.'

crumble beneath the might of their business acumen... or so it would have been, if certain modern theories concerning the shape of the world had not proved to be so disastrously wrong...

I was annoyed with him (Gilliam) because he went over budget and instead of producing what we'd asked for, which I think was seven minutes, I think he produced twenty-three! I thought he was capable of being completely overtaken by his artistic ego and losing boundaries almost completely. And I felt annoyed with John Goldstone, the producer, that John would not restrain him. (John Cleese)

And so on to the main feature, as the screen is suddenly filled with several very strange-looking fish swimming about in a large tank. Each fish has a humanoid face – a Python's face, to be exact. These are incredibly rare 'comedy fish', whose regular morning ritual has just been ruined on account of one of their shoal, 'Howard', currently lying upon a platter with nothing more than a sprig of parsley to hide his modesty.

While the comedy fish are left to mourn Howard's demise and ponder their shallow existence, we segue nicely into the movie's opening credits, which are once again accompanied by a catchy song sung inimitably by Eric Idle and a phantasmagoria of bizarre images culled from the bowels of Gilliam's warped imagination. These images include a perplexed God seen examining two earths (one of which is circular while the other is cube-shaped); a well-rounded naked lady, who appears to be modelling the cloud she's holding above her head into some sort of wig, whilst an elderly lady clutching a handful of balloons is seen approaching from the east; a large Buddha who is floating around in space before being swallowed up by an orbiting space house, which is home to a team of suburban astronauts who are then gobbled up by a runaway express train which then hurtles into a massed bank of filing cabinets, one of which is filled with copy upon copy of Leonardo Da Vinci's 'Vitruvian Man'; a demonic dragon with a detachable head; and a blue-skinned couch potato whose lifeblood slowly seeps through a drain and down into an enormous machine that mass-produces replica clones of the average family complete with the obligatory 2.6 children. But what does it all mean...?

It's... 'The Meaning of Life', apparently...

THE MIRACLE OF BIRTH
An anxious, expectant Mrs Moore (Valerie Whittington), whose contractions are becoming more and more frequent, lies atop a hospital

Trivia Fact: The 'Find the Fish' segment was meant to represent the role of dreams in life, but was inadequately explained.

Trivia Fact: During the title sequence, the title of the movie is first written as 'The Meaning of Liff', and is corrected in a second by a lightning strike. This appears to allude to the humorous dictionary *The Meaning of Liff* (by Douglas Adams and John Lloyd), released in the same year as the movie. The Pythons say they didn't know a book existed bearing that name. – From Wikipedia.com

gurney which is hurtling down a long corridor towards the 'Foetus Frightening Room', where the obstetrician (Chapman) and Dr Spenser (Cleese) are waiting to cure her. Before the curing can commence, however, the good doctor insists that they roll out the expensive equipment, such as the E.E.G., the B.P. Monitor, the A.V.V. and, most importantly, the machine that goes 'ping', which is outrageously expensive as it lets the doctor know that the newborn is still alive.

The equipment is packed into every conceivable space, so much so, in fact, that there's no room for the father-to-be. But there's still something missing... the patient.

"What do I do?" asks the mother-to-be, after being loaded onto the table and having her legs unceremoniously spread akimbo.

"Nothing," replies the good doctor, "you're not qualified."

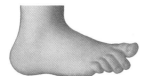

Trivia Fact: The credits for *Meaning of Life* include the disclaimer 'The producers would like to thank all the fish who have taken part in this film. We hope that other fish will follow the example of those who have participated, so that, in future, fish all over the world will live together in harmony and understanding, and put aside their petty differences, cease pursuing and eating each other and live for a brighter, better future for all fish, and those who love them.'

And here comes the dickie-bowed administrator, Mr Pycroft (Palin), who happily explains to the expectant mother how the 'pinging' machine has been leased back from the company that they sold it to so that the cost comes under the monthly current budget, and not the capital account. Not only is Pycroft on hand to explain how the NHS is frittering away the British taxpayers' money, he's also there to learn the more technical aspects of the medical profession, such as a 'birth' being when the doctors take a new baby out of a lady's tummy.

The contractions are coming thick and fast now, so it's 'eyes down for a full house', and don't forget to amplify the pinging machine. Once the baby has been sufficiently frightened, and wrapped in rough towels, it is then shown to the mother, who naturally enquires as to her offspring's sex. The obstetrician, however, admonishes Mrs Moore for attempting to impose roles on one so young and delicate, and after a word of warning about the dangers of the totally-irrational 'P.N.D.', he informs her that she is eligible for prescription-free 'happy pills', and will also be able to purchase a video recording of the birth, which is available on Betamax, VHS and Super 8.

(Ping.)

THE MIRACLE OF BIRTH, PART TWO
We must travel over Ilkley Moor to deepest darkest Yorkshire, a Third World county which is apparently in danger of collapse – not from the myriad of mining tunnels deep below the cobbled surface, but from

the ever-increasing Catholic horde. Although there are no doubt many large families of the Catholic persuasion living within the shadow of the White Rose, we will concentrate on but one such family, who have so many offspring that they make the shoe-dwelling old woman of the fabled nursery rhyme seem in need of fertility treatment.

As we arrive upon the family's over-congested domicile, which is about to become even more cramped on account of the bundle-bearing stork that is nestled upon the roof, Mum (Jones) is beavering away at the kitchen sink, while the flat-capped patriarch (Palin) is returning home with a heavy heart. The reason for his melancholic state is that the mill, which has provided years of gainful employment so that he

Trivia Fact: In this scene, Michael Palin sung "those little rubber things on the end of my sock" in order not to offend the sensitive ears of the child actors around him. The key word was dubbed in later.

could put food upon the table, has closed down, leaving him with little option but to sell his brood for medical experiments. He blames this untimely misfortune not on the mill owner for having failed to attract new customers for his goods, or even the government for having failed to stem the flood of cheap foreign imported goods, but on the Catholic Church, which may have preserved the might, majesty and mystery of the Church of Rome, the sanctity of the sacraments and the indivisible Oneness of the Trinity, but wouldn't allow him to put a 'little rubber thingy' on the end of his cock.

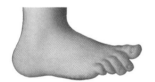

Trivia Fact: Several films are directly spoofed in *Meaning of Life*, including *The Crimson Pirate*, *The Seventh Seal*, *The Exterminating Angel*, *Zulu*, *Mary Poppins*, *The Sound of Music* and *Oliver!*

The situation might not have been so grim had Mum been able to at least wear a pessary on occasion, but the insertion of a medicated vaginal suppository would have resulted in excommunication from the world's fastest growing religion. This is the cue for the family to segue into a musical number that emphasizes the merits of the humble sperm, while aided and abetted by a chorus line consisting of neighbouring miners in outhouses, nannies with babies and the local undertakers (with their client).

With the musical interlude seemingly at an end, a solemn-looking procession of urchins is seen filing out of the house with one-way tickets to the nearest biomedical test centre, as the pious and fully-fledged card-carrying Protestant Harry Blackitt (Chapman) is chastising his Catholic neighbour, albeit via Mrs Blackitt (Idle), for having wilfully "filled the world up with people that he can't afford to bloody feed!" When Harry enlightens his wife as to the reason why his neighbour has so many offspring, she concludes that it must be the same for Protestants because their having two children equates to the number of times they've had sexual intercourse.

But that's not the point, as Harry readily points out, for thanks to Martin Luther having nailed his protest to the Church's door in 1517, he, as could any other male Protestant, can pop down to the local pharmaceutical dispensary and purchase a condom to place upon his 'John Thomas'. And not just any condom either. For should Harry be so inclined he could purchase a 'French Tickler', a 'Black Mambo' or even a 'Crocodile Rib'; sheaths that are designed not only to protect but also to enhance the stimulation of sexual congress.

This earth-shattering, and potentially life-enhancing, discovery is enough for the sexually dormant Mrs Blackitt to put aside her knitting and enquire as to why her spouse hasn't bothered to pop down to the aforementioned dispensary to purchase that special 'something for the weekend' in recent years. But the fault for years of conjugal neglect lies not at Harry's door, but with the Catholic Church for being stuck in the Middle Ages, and also the domination of alien Episcopal supremacy. But despite the attempts of Protestants to promote the idea of sex for pleasure, children continued to multiply everywhere...

GROWTH AND LEARNING

As schools are associated with both growth and learning, it is perhaps not too surprising that the next segment of the movie is set in such an establishment – albeit a public one. We need to be very quiet, for the headmaster, the venerable Humphrey Williams (Cleese), is giving the pupils a lesson on camel-spotting before the third hour, and also how the Midianites went forth to Ram Gilead in Kadesh Bilgemath, by Shor Ethra Regalion, to the house of Gash-Bil-Bethuel-Bazda, who had apparently brought the butter dish to Balshazar, and the tent peg to the house of Rashomon, and whilst there slew the goats and placed the pieces in a pot.

Once the chaplain (Palin) has praised and toadied up to the Lord, Headmaster Humphrey informs the congregation that two boys had been caught dousing the school's pet cormorant in linseed oil, which evidently merited greater concern than one of the pupil's mothers having died earlier in the day. Humphrey is taking a very dim view of the whole affair on account of the unfortunate, and now highly pungent, bird having been presented to the school by the Sudbury Town Corporation in order to commemorate Empire Day, the day when the school would try to remember the names of all those from Sudbury that had so gallantly laid down their lives so that China could remain British.

Trivia Fact: The school used in this segment was the Royal Masonic School of Bushey (which was closed in 1977 to become the International University of Europe, and is often used as a film location).

To conclude, the chaplain, masters and pupils all strike up the school song, which beseeches the good Lord not to burn, grill, toast, barbecue, simmer, braise, bake, boil, stir-fry, poach, baste, fricassee, roast, boil or place them, his servants, in a Rotissomat.

It was a funny experience, Meaning of Life. I really felt more separated because I was in my own little world, hopping in occasionally to do something in the other. We were no longer working like a tight unit, like on Brian. I think by Meaning of Life, the writing was much more separate, everyone was doing their own thing more, and then we just stitched it together. (Terry Gilliam)

Before Humphrey can begin with the first lesson of the day, he first explains that should any of the pupils be participating in that afternoon's match they must move their uniforms down to the lower peg before lunch, and also before writing any letters home. They must do this unless they aren't getting their hair cut, or should they happen to have a younger brother who is going out for the weekend as the guest of another boy. In which case they should collect his (the brother's) note before lunch and place the note in with their letter, but only after having a haircut, and then instruct said brother to move the aforementioned uniform onto the lower peg.

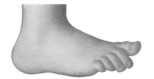

Trivia Fact: The Director's Cut of the film includes three extra scenes, including 'The Adventures of Martin Luther', which directly follows on after the scene with the Protestant couple discussing birth control; a promotional film about the British army which follows the marching scene and a third of Eric Idle and Michael Palin talking about tampons.

Confused? So is young Wymer (Chapman), whose younger brother is due to go out with his friend Dibble, but he, himself, is uncertain as to whether he should still move his clothes down to the lower peg as he's not in need of a haircut. How Wymer can fail to grasp something so simple is beyond Humphrey, but he must be feeling generous, in spite of what happened to the cormorant, as he patiently explains again that Wymer, if not having a haircut, has no need to move his brother's clothes down to the lower peg. He should, however, collect his brother's note before lunch, and after he, himself, has finished his scripture prep. He should then write a letter home; then, and only then, should he look to move his own clothes onto the lower hook, before prepping the visitors, and then report to Mr Viney to confirm that he's had his chitty signed.

Although we suspect young Wymer is still none the wiser, he decides to let the matter rest, as the lesson about to commence is on sex education. Humphrey, upon discovering that the class has yet to broach the topic of how the penis enters the vagina, takes them through a quick recap of 'foreplay', which, much to Wymer's chagrin, isn't just about removing one's clothing and placing it on the lower peg, but is in fact the collective term used for the various methods of lubricating a female vagina so that the male penis can enter more

easily. Once this has been explained he engages the pupils to name two means of getting them (the vaginal juices) flowing, and elicits several enlightening responses in return such as "rubbing the clitoris", "sucking the nipple", "stroking the thighs" and "biting the neck".

The lesson is interrupted when Humphrey's wife, Helen, enters the classroom, but it's a nice interruption, as interruptions go, for she proceeds, as does Humphrey, to strip off before clambering upon the drop-down four-poster bed to await the next lesson: penetration and coitus. Humphrey then proceeds to mount his good lady wife whilst providing a running commentary for the pupils, who had all better pay attention, as he has no intention of going through it all again. One pupil, by the name of Biggs (Jones), is unable to contain his mirth at seeing Mr and Mrs Humphrey 'in flagrante' as it were, and as a punishment is selected (or maybe that should be sentenced) to play for the boys' team in that afternoon's rugby match against the masters. Needless to say, by the end of the match, or ritualized slaughter, the diminutive Biggs is left battered, bruised and in need of a mug of matron's hot cocoa, but alas this is not to be, for his services are needed for the next segment:

FIGHTING EACH OTHER

Biggs is suddenly propelled forward through time to find himself an officer serving in the British Army during the Great War of 1914-18. He and his small band of loyal and dedicated men are making their way across no-man's land on a mission to take out the enemy's machine guns – but when the good captain gives the order for his men to separate, Private Blackitt (Idle), who may well be a distant relation to the God-fearing Protestant from an earlier sketch, insists that they should stick together. Biggs is obviously very fond of his men, but an order is an order and Blackitt reluctantly agrees. However, before he, Sturridge (Cleese) and Walters (Gilliam) depart to take out the "buggers on the left", he announces that he and the rest of the chaps have had a whip-around and bought their captain a nice carriage clock. Timepieces must have been in abundance in war-torn France, for the men also present the good captain with a grandfather clock, which was on account of there being a bit of a mix-up between the lads. Sturridge, apparently oblivious to what his chums were doing, has bought his captain a very nice wristwatch, which is apparently Swiss, and as if these unexpected gifts weren't enough, Blackitt also mentions that the lads have got him a card – which is apparently blood-splattered, but it's the thought that counts. Biggs is naturally overwhelmed at his subordinates' generosity, but daylight is wasting and there is still the matter of the German guns

Trivia Fact: John Cleese starred as gadgetmaster 'Q' in the recent James Bond films *Die Another Day* and *The World is Not Enough.*

to attend to, but that is no excuse for losing his temper when Blackitt mentions something about a cheque, which Spadger (Palin), what with all the excitement, has unfortunately left behind in trench number four.

A line has now been crossed, and the men are somewhat reluctant to present Biggs with the cake which Blackitt had not only baked, regardless of the difficulties he encountered trying to get butter to melt at fifteen degrees below freezing, but had even forgone six weeks of rations in order to do so. The good captain, now feeling somewhat ashamed at having appeared ungrateful, abandons the mission in favour of sampling the cake and orders Private Walters to dish out the knives and plates. Walters is prevented from carrying out the order on account of getting himself shot, as does Private Sturridge, but all is not lost, however, as the very efficient Private Hordern is on hand to take over with laying out the tablecloth, and even has the forethought to fetch two doilies should one happen to get crumpled.

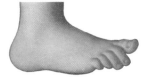

Trivia Fact: Ruling out a Monty Python reunion to the press in January 2006, Eric Idle stated "We're all over sixty and comedy is really a young man's game and it's sort of about what you had to say when you were fresh and young. I'm perfectly happy to get drunk with the rest of them. I was just in London and we had a really spectacular dinner, but I think it really should go no further than that. We've earned that."

It's not a general rule, because I think there were things we did in The Meaning of Life *– for instance, the 'Sperm Song' – which we couldn't have done unless we had some money. And that was a really good use of money; whereas before it would have been just a neat idea, we made it into something with quite a towering impression, a sequence to stand in comparison with the best Hollywood musical sequences. And you could only do that with a bit of money.* (Michael Palin)

Whether Captain Biggs and his dwindling number survive the ongoing German bombardment long enough to have their cake and eat it too shall remain a mystery, for they are consigned to history as a modern-day general (Chapman) appears on screen to inform us that warfare isn't all fun and games. For although it may well be considered amusing in some quarters to poke fun at the military, when one stops to consider that the meaning of life is a struggle between alternative viewpoints of life itself, and that without the ability to defend one's own viewpoint against other perhaps more aggressive ideologies, then reasonableness and moderation could quite simply disappear. That, the general goes on to insist, is why we – the British nation – will always need an army, and may God strike him down if it were to be otherwise.

(Ziff boom.)

The general, having slipped his frazzled mortal coil, is suitably replaced by a zealous sergeant major (Palin) who, after berating his men for not having previously witnessed the hand of God in action, goes on to inform

them that they can look forward to an afternoon of good old fashioned marching up and down the parade ground. That is, of course, unless they should happen to have something better to do.

Trivia Fact: In the trench warfare sequence, Biggs is given a clock which is then placed on the ridge. In the next shot, it is gone.

Private Atkinson (Idle), upon revealing that he would rather be at home with the wife and kids, is suitably discharged, as is Private Coles (Chapman), who apparently has a book he'd quite like to read. When Private Wyclif (Andrew MacLachlan) elects to get in a spot of piano practice, the sergeant major enquires as to whether the rest of his squad wouldn't rather be enjoying themselves at the cinema. Needless to say, Merle Oberon wins hands down and the sergeant major is left to march alone.

Democracy and humanitarianism have, despite what the sergeant major may think, always been the trademarks of the British Army, which has stamped its triumph throughout history in the furthest-flung corners of the Empire. But no matter where or when there was fighting to be done, it has always been the calm leadership of the officer class that has made the British Army what it is.

A fine example of the aforementioned calm leadership was witnessed during the first Zulu War, which did not take place in Glasgow as was first believed, but in Africa's Natal Province, when a certain Major Ainsworth (Cleese) ignored the raging battle taking place a few feet away to finish his morning shave – despite his shaving mirror having been shattered by a stray bullet.

It is perhaps worth taking a brief timeout in order to congratulate the Pythons on their attention to detail in the battle scenes that, upon first glance, wouldn't have looked out of place in the 1964 movie *Zulu*, starring Michael Caine and Stanley Baker.

Unlike Lieutenants Bromhead and Chard, who gallantly defended Rourke's Drift against an overwhelming Zulu force, Major Ainsworth and his fellow officer, Major Pakenham-Walsh (Palin), appear more concerned with mosquitoes getting through their nets at night while they are asleep than anything the Zulus might throw at them. The worst casualty appears to be Major Perkins, who has lost a leg during the night. Perkins is surprisingly nonchalant about having just woken up to discover that he has one sock too many, but his fellow officers are concerned that the blood-thirsty blighters (that's the mosquitoes and not the Zulus) might return for the rest of Perkins' leg and send for Doctor Livingstone (Chapman) who, upon learning that his now-limbless colleague isn't suffering from a headache, and that his bowels are in order, diagnoses a fever and suggests that Perkins should keep warm and get plenty of rest, and that, should he want to play football, he may want to favour his other leg.

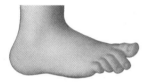

Trivia Fact: Eric Idle remarked to the *Los Angeles Times* in 1996 that "I don't think we'll ever escape the curse of Python. I feel it's like [a] snake with [a] hat on... We'd really rather hide, but it's rather a large snake."

When Perkins enquires as to whether his missing limb will grow back on its own account, however, the good doctor decides to come clean, and informs his patient that he isn't suffering from a fever at all, as fevers tend to be quite small and therefore couldn't have possibly made off with a whole leg. He then makes what he stresses is little more than an educated guess in that his fellow officer has fallen foul of an eleven-foot-long multi-cellular lifeform with stripes and huge razor-sharp teeth, and which is of the genus 'Felis Horribilis' – or what he, and other doctors, in fact call a 'tiger'.

"A tiger... in Africa?" This startling revelation is enough to wipe out most of the soldiers and sends the Zulus scampering back to their kraals.

It is at this point that a bloodied and battle-weary sergeant (Jones) arrives to inform the officers that the attack is over and that the Zulus are retreating. The victory, however, has come at a high price, for 'Signals' are gone, thirty men from 'F' Section have been killed and 'C' Division has been wiped out altogether, but 150 casualties apparently pales into insignificance when compared to the possibility that there may be a tiger... in Africa.

Even one that has escaped from a zoo!

Upon learning that Major Perkins' leg, if located immediately, could in fact be reattached, the sergeant volunteers to organise a party but is admonished by his superiors for his supposed insensitivity. The sergeant is spared from being placed on report, however, by explaining that it was actually a 'search party' that he was intending to muster and not a cocktail party, although I'm sure that permission to organise such a soirée amid the dead and dying rank and 'offal' would have been considered a spiffing idea had it not been for Perkins' inability to do the foxtrot on account of his missing leg.

Everything that was good about Life of Brian *was bad about* Meaning of Life. Life of Brian, *we knew instinctively what we were writing about, everybody was writing well, the story developed remarkably easily and organically, we knew that we were on to something good and funny and meaningful, and the shooting process was a joy – except the last few days, when I got a rotten chest infection – I remember saying to someone, "Being crucified is bad enough, it's no fun when you have the flu as well."* (John Cleese)

The hastily assembled search party sets off into the surrounding jungle to, well, search for the limb-snaffling tiger. Upon reaching a clearing the party comes upon a huge striped beast and opens fire, so imagine their surprise (although perhaps nothing should come as a 'surprise' when the Pythons are involved) when the 'tiger' turns out to be a pantomime tiger, the front end of which (Idle) begs the officers not to shoot for he and his lower half (Palin) are in fact on a mission for British Intelligence and have dressed up as a tiger in order to seek out a pro-Tsarist Ashanti Chief.

"Oh no they're not!"

No, they're not. Neither are they making an advertisement for 'Tiger' brand coffee, despite the impromptu catchy jingle that claims

Trivia Fact: John Cleese was the first Python to become a grandparent when his daughter Cynthia Cleese gave birth to a boy, Evan Daniel, in March 1997. The father, screenwriter Ed Solomon, wrote the films *Men in Black* and *Bill and Ted's Excellent Adventure*.

the coffee is 'a real treat that tigers prefer to the taste of meat', nor commemorating the fiftieth anniversary of the front end's auntie, who'd apparently dressed up as a tiger in 1839. Major Atkinson is also sceptical about the front end's explanation that he and his colleague have escaped from a Bengal psychiatric institution and had made the tiger skin out of old, used cereal packets. The reason, no matter how ludicrous or far-fetched for the two men wearing a tiger suit in the middle of the jungle, is a moot point as far as Major Perkins is concerned, however, for all he wants to know is whether they have his leg or not!

And no, not a wooden one!

In a continuity error, when the search party is seen walking through the forest, two Zulu POWs can be seen carrying the front end of Perkins' bed, while a soldier and Doctor Livingstone are carrying it from the rear. But when the party emerge out into the clearing, the two Zulus are nowhere to be seen, and it is the soldier and the doctor who are carrying the front end of the bed.

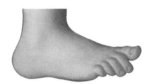

Trivia Fact: The green elephant-esque troll costume used in the sketch was a leftover and unused costume from Gilliam's *Time Bandits*, made in 1981.

Upon hearing Atkinson's order for his man to search the surrounding thicket, the front end (who must be an officer of sorts for he is wearing epaulettes on his undershirt), attempts to bluff his way out by asking if he and his chum look like the sort of chaps who would creep into a camp at night, steal into someone's tent, anaesthetize them, tissue-type them, amputate a leg and then run off with it. Major Ainsworth, however, remains unconvinced, and with good reason, for it appears that there is indeed a leg lurking within the thicket, although it was apparently abandoned by someone else who was probably miles away by this time, leaving Messrs front- and rear-end to take the blame as usual.

Just when you thought it couldn't get any sillier, a pantomime Zulu (Gilliam) unzips his costume to announce that... tun, tara-tun, tara-tun, tun, tun, ta... we have reached the 'Middle of the Film'.

I think there was a general sense that it had not been a very satisfactory experience, and while I don't remember a conscious decision being made not to make another film, I think it was like when you go to a restaurant that isn't very good: You don't actually say, "I'm never going back there again," you just suddenly discover three years later that you've never been drawn back. I think it was like that. (John Cleese)

An elegantly dressed lady presenter (Palin) welcomes us to the middle of the movie, the time when the filmmakers invite the audience to 'find the fish'. This involves watching a scene from another movie and then trying to guess where the fish is, and if we should happen to already know the location of the concealed fish, then we are invited to yell out so that everyone else within the cinema can hear us.

Trying to spot the aforementioned 'fish' is the furthest thing from the viewer's mind upon seeing a bizarre-looking man (Jones) who resembles a French waiter with elongated arms, an equally-bizarre female (Chapman) who looks as though he's an extra from *The Rocky Horror Picture Show* and a silent green elephant-esque-headed waiter-type troll (Mark Holmes). The two cavort to background music while the man ponders where the elusive fish, which he apparently loved like a son, and which followed him wherever he did go, could possibly be hiding.

Trivia Fact: According to interviews, the 'meaning of life' concept was evidently the best way the Python team came up with for tying together a movie of otherwise unrelated sketches.

While certain members of the 'staged audience' offer suggestions that the fishy, fishy fish is hidden up the elephant-esque creature's trunk, or within his trousers, the camera pans to the fish tank first seen at the beginning of the movie, which contains the Python-fish. Although they are in biased agreement that this sketch is the best bit of the entire movie, they appear to be slightly perplexed as to why nothing has been said about the meaning of life.

Oh, here we go...

MIDDLE AGE

The next sketch invites us to join a middle-aged American couple, Mr and Mrs Marvin Hendy (Palin and Idle respectively) who, after Mrs Hendy has performed a special favour for her husband on account of 'it' having been 'misty', enter a restaurant where they encounter the elegant M'lady Joeline (Gilliam). Joeline, upon learning that the Hendys are quite partial to pineapples, suggests that they might like to be seated within the Dungeon Room, which offers real Hawaiian food, served in an authentic, medieval English dungeon atmosphere.

The Hendys are escorted to their table, but like the majority of middle-aged married couples that one sees in restaurants throughout the land, they appear incapable of making conversation. The embarrassing silence is brought to an end, however, with the timely arrival of the waiter (Cleese), who's dressed in a garish red-checked sports jacket and sporting an equally garish crew-cut, and who hands them a menu that provides a whole multitude of conversational topics, including tonight's specialty – 'minorities'.

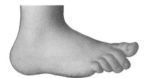

Trivia Fact: During the 'Find the Fish' sequence, a camera can be seen onscreen.

Mrs Hendy peruses the menu and enquires as to one particular specialty but is somewhat less than inclined to engage her husband in a conversation on the forthcoming Steelers-Bears football game, or to reminisce about a previous great 'World Series'.

She then enquires as to another mouth-watering delicacy – 'philosophy', which, she's glad to hear, isn't a sport, but actually more of an attempt to construct a valid hypothesis on the meaning of life (ba-doom-tish).

So philosophy for two it is then, but the Hendys appear incapable of starting off such a conversation. The waiter, however, no doubt having encountered similar tongue-tied couples before, offers to kick-start the conversation for them by enquiring as to whether either of them has ever wondered why they are here.
Mr Hendy is off the blocks now and informs the waiter that they are 'here' because he and his good lady had vacationed in Miami the previous year, and in California the year before that.

No, no, no, philosophizing isn't about perusing travel brochures for suitable holiday destinations, but about trying to unravel the mysteries of human existence.

The waiter, with other middle-aged couples in urgent need of conversational stimulation, hands the Hendys some conversation cue cards containing the names of philosophers such as Schopenhauer, the one whose name begins with the letter 's', and Nietzsche, whose name, although not actually beginning with the serpentine letter, does contain the letter therein which Mrs Hendy is led to believe to be a prerequisite for all philosophers.

Selina Jones, although having a name that begins with the letter 's', and known for having sung about the meaning of life, sadly doesn't qualify for philosophizership on account of her having had to rely on Burt Bacharach for her material. Burt, despite being the kingfish around town when it comes to composing memorable tunes, also fails to qualify on account of his moniker being sans 's'. Whether he would be allowed by proxy on account of his being married to Carole Bayer Sager, who does have the prerequisite 's', is a moot point, not to mention mind-numbingly boring, and the Hendys quite rightly abandon philosophizing in favour, or should that be 'flavour', of the house specialty – liver transplants.

LIVE ORGAN TRANSPLANTS

Mr Brown (Gilliam), an unsuspecting everyday sort of chap, opens his front door to find two white-coated gentlemen (Chapman and Cleese) standing upon his doorstep. It would seem that they are door-to-door organ removal specialists who have come to remove the large reddish-brown glandular organ that is secreted within his abdomen on account of him being the proud owner of a liver-donor card.

Mr Brown tries to protest on the grounds that the donor card states that his liver is to be removed 'in the event of death', and that he's still sort of using it, but the removal men have no time for lightweight excuses and inform their victim, I mean patient, that the hour of his demise is at hand – for none of their other patients have survived the procedure.

Mrs Brown (Jones) appears more upset with having her cosy front room transformed into a slaughterhouse than finding two strangers slicing and dicing her spouse for their glandular prize, and blames her husband for having returned from the local library filled with good intentions, and in possession of one of those 'silly cards'. She's also had enough of listening to his screaming and offers to put the kettle on. One of the men, who has already admitted that neither he, nor his blood-splattered colleague, are actually doctors, attempts to engage the soon-to-be widowed Mrs Brown in a spot of courtship, but upon

Trivia Fact: Speaking about the writing of *Meaning of Life* to Empire magazine in 1997, John Cleese said "I probably owe my life to the fact that I couldn't get the rest of them to vote for my material. Graham and I wrote this savage attack on the Ayatollah Khomeini, about this frenzied loony with all these religious objections to toilet paper. It was just a scurrilous, way over-the-top attack on Islamic extremists. I thought it was hilarious, and the others didn't, so it never got in. And I owe my life to that, because we would've got at least a fatwah each. Actually, maybe that's what happened to Graham..."

hearing that she "is too old for that sort of thing" abandons his plans to take her hand and asks for her liver instead. When Mrs Brown appears apprehensive, and why shouldn't she be given what is taking place in the adjoining room, the man attempts to allay her fears with a little light entertainment provided by a pink-suited crooner (Idle), who emerges from the Browns' humble refrigerator. The wannabe Liberace waves his magic cane, obliterates the kitchen wall and invites Mrs Brown to accompany him on a delightful stroll through the amazing and expanding universe, which is enough to see her relent and agree to part with her liver.

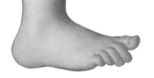

Trivia Fact: The 'meaning of life' espoused by Harry in the meeting of the board of the Very Big Corporation of America, that a soul must be brought into existence by a process of guided self-observation, is a common theme throughout many of the world's esoteric spiritual traditions, such as Sufism and Tantra. It is particularly close to the teaching of the Russian mystic G. I. Gurdjieff, who posited that man is asleep and can only wake up through consistent effort at self-remembering.

Time, however, is of the essence, and we must abandon Mrs Brown to her fate and set sail across the High Accountan-cy to return to the financial district that we first saw in the featurette presentation. As the sign writer can be seen adding 'Liver Donors, Inc.' to the conglomerate's list of companies, the chairman (Chapman) calls the board's attention to item six on the agenda: the meaning of life.

Harry (Palin), who has apparently given some thought to the matter, informs his colleagues that the meaning of life can in fact be reduced to two fundamental concepts. First, that people are not wearing enough hats, and second, that matter is energy. Harry then launches into a hypothesis on there being many energy fields within our universe, which we, humans, cannot normally perceive; some of which have a spiritual source which act upon a person's soul. However, the 'soul' does not exist *ab initio*, as Orthodox Christianity would have us believe, and has in fact to be brought into existence by a process of self-guided observation. This phenomenon, however, is rarely achieved on account of man's unique ability to be distracted from spiritual matters by everyday trivia.

CHAPTER SEVEN

"What was that about the hats again?"

The debate on whether hat sales have increased is interrupted by Gunther (Idle) who, in reference to Harry's second point, draws everyone's attention to the foreboding-looking building that can now be seen through the window. It's the piratical Crimson Permanent Assurance, but just as battle is about to commence the projectionist steps in to interrupt proceedings and apologizes for the unwarranted attack by the supporting feature. Luckily for us, not to mention the corporate bigwigs, the production team is prepared for this eventuality and takes the necessary steps to remedy the situation.

THE AUTUMN YEARS

And so we are transported to a sedate restaurant where Noel Coward (Idle) is serenading the clientele with a little ditty about the male penis that he happened to 'toss off' whilst holidaying in the Caribbean. The song draws to a close and as the diners are offering their appreciation, one of the Python fish alerts us to the arrival of Mr Creosote (Jones) whose enormous girth is equal to that of a sperm whale. The maître d' (Cleese) escorts his portly guest to a nearby table and orders Gaston (Idle), in a ridiculously exaggerated French accent, to bring a sick bucket for the Monsieur, before enticing Mr Creosote with his favourite dish, which is "ze jugged hare" within a rich sauce comprising of truffles, anchovies, Grand Marnier, bacon and cream. Mr Creosote, however, has not yet finished disgorging the contents of his Shea Stadium-sized gut and proceeds to fill a new hastily-brought bucket while the maître d' rhymes off the appetizers, which include moules marinières, pâté de foie gras, beluga caviar and eggs Benedictine, amongst others. He needn't have bothered, as Mr Creosote normally orders everything on the menu served in a bucket (hopefully not the 'vomit' one) with eggs on top, and washes it down with six bottles of the Château Latour Forty-Five, a double jeroboam of Champagne and six crates of brown ale – and no skimping on the pâté!

Creosote was quite hard. I was a bit nervous about doing that, actually; originally I said Terry Gilliam ought to do it, and then Terry persuaded me that I ought to do it. I was a bit worried because it was a big make-up job, three and a half hours. And, of course, the biggest thing was to get the vomit to look real. I didn't want it to squirt out, I wanted it to sort of 'bludge' out – go 'blurp'! We had a device, a tube that didn't go into my mouth, it was at the side of the mouth, and I had to be at an absolute right angle. It looked fine when we tested it and everything, we shot the first day, and then we went to see the rushes, and it didn't work. What we hadn't realised was that

Trivia Fact: The sequence in which Graham Chapman is chased to his death features music from *Monty Python and the Holy Grail*.

when the liquid came out of the side, there was a shadow from my face on the liquid, so you saw it wasn't coming out of my mouth. (Terry Jones)

Meanwhile, the harried Gaston has arrived with a replacement bucket, and only just in the nick of time, as Creosote, with soda-siphon precision, vomits into the bucket and also onto the unfortunate cleaning lady. Several of the nearby guests are splattered with vomit, and when one couple (Chapman and Cleveland) gets up to leave, the husband first assures the maître d' that their reason for doing so is that they have a train to catch, and his heavily-menstruating wife will first need to attend to herself to avoid bleeding all over the seats.

Hmm.

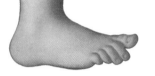

Trivia Fact: The 'Mr Creosote' sequence was originally rejected by almost all of the Pythons, before later being rescued by John Cleese, who had decided that it was the funniest part!

It was work habits that had changed. We weren't all at the same level trying to work just for the show. I mean, lifestyles were getting in the way: "I'm a Hollywood star, I need this…" It's not that one is right or wrong, it's just they're different ways of working. Work habits – that's the only way I can describe it. (Terry Gilliam)

I think the fact was that we'd struggled for a long time to get a script together, we were writing from almost as soon as we'd done Brian. *And there was tons of stuff, far more material was thrown away during the writing of* Meaning of Life *than any other thing we'd done on Python. Tons of stuff just didn't quite work out.* (Michael Palin)

Jones, in the 'Making of' documentary, reveals how the extras used in this scene were all clamouring for the honour of being struck by the vomit (which was actually cold Minestrone soup), and one can imagine them squabbling as so and so deserved the right as they had worked on *Life of Brian*, while others argued how they deserved it more for having worked with Olivier at the 'Vic'.

Mr Creosote is left to gorge in peace, and judging from the pile of plates and dishes stacked upon the table before him at the end of the evening, what a gargantuan gorge it was, too. The maître d', however, has one more treat in store for his favourite customer in the form of a wafer-thin mint. This proves to be the proverbial straw that crippled the camel, or perhaps a better analogy would be the spark that ignited the Hindenburg, for like the ill-feted airship the rapidly expanding Mr Creosote explodes, sending a tidal wave of vomit cascading through the restaurant.

THE MEANING OF LIFE

The restaurant is now closed, and while the waiters are scrubbing and scraping the eviscerated Mr Creosote's remains from the floor, ceiling and walls, the maître d' confesses to Maria the cleaning lady (Jones) that he doubts that he will ever find the true meaning of life working in a restaurant. Maria, however, although a humble cleaner, is more philosophical, and not because she has dined with the Hendys, but rather for having worked at the Académie Française, the Prado in Madrid, the Library of Congress and the Bodleian Library, though she had learned nothing about life's great mystery and had developed arthritis and strained her eyes in the bargain. She refuses to be bitter, though, for she views life as a game that can be either won or lost from time to time, and although she's feeling down right now, at least she doesn't work for Jews.

The maître d', in an attempt to avoid being sued by the state of Israel, grabs up the vomit bucket and dumps it on Maria's head before apologizing profusely about having been unaware that he had employed a racist. *Quel dommage!*

Gaston, who has obviously seen enough puke to last a lifetime, invites us to accompany him on a journey that he believes will help to unravel the mystery of the meaning of life. We follow him down a flight of stairs, across a Zebra crossing, along the high street and through a park, until at last we arrive upon the quaint little cottage where he was born. It was here, he explains, that his dear mother placed the young Gaston upon her knee and told him how the world was a beautiful place and that he should learn to love his fellow man, or woman (thank you, Stan/Loretta),

Trivia Fact: The line "Hey, I didn't even eat the mousse," spoken by Michael Palin in the 'Death' segment, is one of the few ad-libs in any Python effort.

The End?

The Pythons are often the subject of reunion rumours. The death of Graham Chapman in 1989 (on the eve of their twentieth anniversary) seemed to put an end to this speculation, but in 1998 the five remaining members, along with what was purported to be Chapman's ashes, were reunited on stage for the first time in eighteen years. The occasion was in the form of an interview (hosted by Robert Klein, with an appearance by Eddie Izzard) in which the team looked back at some of their work and performed a few new skits. At one point during the event, Chapman's urn was 'accidentally' spilled, and the ashes were cleared away with a vacuum cleaner.

On 9 October 1999, to commemorate thirty years since the Flying Circus' first TV appearance, BBC2 devoted an evening to Python programmes, including a documentary charting the history of the team, interspersing them with new sketches filmed especially for the event.

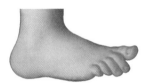

Trivia Fact: A new species of snake was discovered in Australia in the early 1980s, of which the Latin name starts Monty Python... The full name: Montypythonsidesriversleighensis.
– From Wikipedia.com

make everyone happy, whilst attempting to bring peace and contentment wherever he should go. Well, he's right about one thing: It is a pretty shitty philosophy, but "I can live my own life in my own way if I want to. Fuck off."

DEATH

Amid the sound of crashing waves, seagulls and suspenseful music, we watch Arthur Charles Herbert Runcie MacAdam Jarrett (Chapman) who, having been convicted by twelve good men and found guilty of the crime of first degree making of gratuitous, sexist jokes in a motion picture, is about to die. He has, however, been allowed to choose the manner of his own demise, which sees him being chased over the edge of a cliff by a bevy of semi-naked buxom beauties who are wearing boots, kneepads, crash helmets and not much else.

This is followed by one of Gilliam's more bizarre animation shorts, involving a tree losing its suicidal leaves. Hmm, not sure about the meaning of this one, Mr G. But then again, that's the point, surely.

Cue more music, only this time the tune is a haunting one for death, in the form of the Grim Reaper (Cleese) walking amongst us. Today the Reaper's scythe has come for Geoffrey (Chapman), his wife Angela (Idle), their dinner guests Howard and Debbie Katzenberg (Gilliam and Palin), who hail from Philadelphia, and Jeremy and Fiona Portland-Smythe (Simon and Terry Jones).

Geoffrey is slightly puzzled at the unwarranted intrusion, for although the garden hedge is somewhat overgrown, he has no particular need for any reaping. Angela, however, is anxious that the Reaper might catch his death from the cold should he be left outside any longer and insists that her husband invite him in. The Reaper, what with being dead and all that, has little need for alcoholic refreshment, nor has he come to enlighten anyone about the possibilities of an 'afterlife'. He then put a total dampener on the proceedings by informing the bemused gathering that he has come for them, and what is occurring is not a potentially positive learning experience, but death – cold, stark, finite death – as in parrot.

It was the only studio picture we did, which means it will never go into profit! (Eric Idle)

Debbie Katzenberg, however, remains unconvinced and poses the question as to how it can be that she and her friends have died at the same time. The Reaper's scythe points towards Angela, who has apparently committed a social faux pas in using canned salmon for her salmon mousse. Well, that explains it, except Debbie didn't actually eat the mousse, but hey, what's one extra? She and the others, along with the also recently-deceased Hendys, arrive at heaven's gate, where a receptionist (Cleveland) informs them that a table has been reserved for them in the restaurant and then wishes them all a happy Christmas (it's Christmas every day in heaven, apparently).

Once the new arrivals have been seated amongst the varied characters from earlier sketches, the celestial entertainment, in the form of a white-suited Tony Bennett (Chapman), can begin. And Bennett wows the crowd with a heartening festive ditty that tells of the joys of Christmas, most notably the movie selection on TV, with *The Sound of Music* being aired twice an hour, and *Jaws* 1, 2 and 3...

Since *The Meaning of Life* opened in cinemas around the world, there have been many press rumours of another Python movie. Possibly the most frequently heard tale is that of a film about the true story of King Arthur, although plenty more have taken its place over the years. With one team member now no longer with us and two ex-Pythons now based permanently in the US, this looks very unlikely, although who knows what effect the runaway success of *Spamalot* on Broadway will have on the remaining team members. Stay tuned.

In an interview to publicise the DVD release of *The Meaning of Life*, Cleese said a further reunion was unlikely. "It is absolutely impossible to get even a majority of us together in a room, and I'm not joking," Cleese said. He said that the problem was one of busyness rather than one of bad feelings. Eric Idle has said that he expects to see a proper Python reunion, "just as soon as Graham Chapman comes back from the dead." (This echoed a comment George Harrison of the Beatles once made: "As far as I'm concerned, there won't be a Beatles reunion as long as John Lennon remains dead.")

The 2003 'autobiography' *The Pythons*, compiled from a series of interviews with the surviving Pythons, reveals that a series of disputes in 1990 over a *Monty Python and the Holy Grail* sequel conceived by Idle may have resulted in the group's permanent fission. Cleese's feeling was that *Monty Python's Meaning of Life* was both personally difficult and ultimately mediocre, and for other reasons, didn't wish to do the film. Apparently Idle was angry with Cleese for refusing to do the film, which most of the remaining Pythons thought reasonably promising. Idle then refused to do what he saw as the Cleese-dominated reunion show a few years later.

Owing in part to the success of *Spamalot*, PBS announced on 13 July 2005, that the network would begin to re-air the entire run of *Monty Python's Flying Circus*, as well as new one-hour specials focusing on each member of the group. Each special is to be written and produced by the individual being honoured, with the five remaining Pythons collaborating on a special for Graham Chapman.

– From *Wikipedia.com*

AFTERWORD: THERE'S NO DEAD WOOD IN REDWOOD...

Andre Jacquemin, who was the engineer involved with all our stuff, worked in his garden shed, and he had a four-track tape recorder and I had my two-track stereo, and we couldn't actually stand up all the way in his shed, so we were all crouching, and we were doing the whole thing like that. (Terry Gilliam)

Looking back on it all now, it was probably Granddad's fault. Let me explain. When my brother David and I were children, we'd often be taken care of by Grandma and Granddad (my Dad's parents) if our parents were out for a meal or some social event. These evenings normally fit into a certain pattern. They would start by us entertaining them with our latest batch of singles (I'm sure they must have loved that! Even at eight or nine we were committed glam rock fans); this would be followed by a board game. My Granddad was a draughts king; he'd play till doomsday! This would go on till late evening – we'd always sneak in late nights when the folks were out, and Grandma would make some hot drinks and get everybody seated around the television. These evenings would normally end in a movie or BBC TV's then-flagship chat show *Parkinson*. On one occasion, Granddad switched on BBC 1, to be greeted by *And Now for Something Completely Different*, which I remember as a zany bunch of crazy un-related sketches, with Eric Idle's 'Nudge Nudge' man having us in fits of laughter.

A few years later, Dad and I were sitting channel hopping – I'd have been about fourteen, and remember Mum was out at a meeting and David was playing football. After coming up with little or nothing on either BBC 1 or ITV, we skipped to BBC 2, and there was Eric Idle in full blown 'Nudge Nudge' mode, only in slightly different surroundings than I'd remembered previously seeing. This, it turned out, was a full-blown re-run of one of the Python TV series. Each week we tuned in, and each week it was more bizarre, incredibly funny and already being repeated verbatim in the schoolyard the next day by the rest of the lads. By the end of the series, I was hooked. I think it was also a good time to discover Monty Python, as *Holy Grail* was already doing cinema reruns (sometimes on double bills with other comedy classics), and the news that *Brian* was just around the corner had been reported just about every week in the music press. Its release also brought about more reason to see it, because none other than the Bishop of Blackburn banned it from our cinema screens. By now we were punk fans, and although we'd have gone to see the movie anyway, its newfound notoriety just sped up the process.

In 1999, Paul Burgess and I collaborated on a book called *Satellite*. To say it was life-changing is an understatement. Suddenly all my dreams were fast becoming a reality. Doors I'd spent years knocking on were falling open at the mere mention of the book's title. I accepted a PR job with my eye on bigger things, and in little or no time I'd met Steve Woof from EMI Records. We shared an interest in some of our music and much of our comedy. I began compiling CDs for the company in 2001; these were largely punk discs, and we would work directly with the artists in question. This meant that the guys I already knew, I got closer to, and those I didn't already know I got to know. One afternoon we were talking about the Monty Python CD catalogue.

"It's far from perfect," I said. "They look like they've been thrown onto CD rather than worked on." Steve explained that in fairness the label they currently existed on, 'Blah Blah Blah Classics', had pretty much been set up to put spoken word vinyl onto CD, nothing fancy, just cheap and cheerful, and the punters could buy them for less than a fiver, so all was good with the situation. We both agreed that a catalogue as important as that of the Pythons' needed some looking into, but beyond that we were both busy on other projects and pretty much left the matter in the office that day.

At the start of summer 2004 I was strolling through Covent Garden with Robert Kirby (my agent) on the way to a meeting. All was well with the world, and so I brought up Python.

"You know," said Robert, "I'm sure one of them is with PFD. I'll find out and let you know." The detective in me went to bed that night sure that we were finally on the trail, itching to move further forward. Robert kept his word and informed me a couple of days later that one of the Pythons was indeed with, or had been with, PFD. I rushed down to their offices to meet another agent, who passed me the number for Python (Monty) Pictures and a man by the name of Roger Saunders. Twenty minutes later, having informed Steve Woof, I was on the phone to Roger. Within a month we had a meeting set at EMI's plush Brook Green offices; now, for the first time, the Monty Python CD catalogue would be given a proper release, bigger booklets, new bonus tracks – if you'll excuse the pun, it was indeed the full Monty!

As a fan, I was aware of Redwood Studios. I knew that Michael Palin had something to do with it – wasn't sure what, but I knew someone had mentioned it, and I knew that Andre Jacquemin was pretty much the George Martin of the Python world. One morning I'd been to collect the mail and came back upstairs to a telephone message from Andre. I rang back instantly and we spoke – at that very moment I knew the project was on. Within a week, Steve Woof and myself were sitting in Redwood discussing all sorts of possibilities. There was, Andre informed us, a wealth of un-issued audio Python that just needed searching for through a mass of studio information papers, known affectionately as 'The Bible' (if you ever see it you'll know why, it'll give that other book of the same title a run for its money size-wise, as I mentioned earlier).

It took Andre and me two days just to go through 'The Bible', never mind actually listening to anything! We started on a Saturday – for about three solid days we listened to un-issued Python (just imagine this if you're a fan), some half-finished sketches, some completed ones and some little more than rough ideas. Every one was (I'll say with my fan hat on firmly) incredibly funny. The tales came along with them as well – a late night recording here, a tape for Lemmy of Motörhead there, a read-through abandoned in favour of a better idea. I always had the Pythons pinned as perfectionists, and it was good to know I'd been right all along.

By the early part of 2005, we had a master plan of sorts. The project would include all eight existing Python albums, along with, for the first time ever, an album of unissued outtakes. Work commenced at Redwood Studios in the heart of London's Soho in February, and since then we've had dinner with Neil Innes, seen the Rutles play live at the 100 Club, spoken to Carol Cleveland on the telephone from

Brighton, been given the greenlight on our *Live at Drury Lane* CD ideas by Terry Gilliam, we've been sparred with by none other than Michael Palin, taken tea with Terry Jones and exchanged numerous funny stories with Bill (Terry's son, who occupies the studio above Redwood) over more coffee! While the team at EMI hit the e-mail and contacted the US to speak with John Cleese and Eric Idle, in all it's the stuff of dreams for someone who would describe themselves as no more than a 100% committed Python nut. On a trip to New York in early December 2005, which included time to promote this very book at a sales convention, the guy who followed us on the podium asked "How do I follow Monty Python?" "You don't!" I shouted, while the rest of the room laughed. It was time for Mick and myself to catch a live performance of *Spamalot*, and by that point I knew the words to every song, thanks to an import copy of the cast recording CD. We had been informed that the Shubert Theatre was situated just off Times Square, but the temperature was below freezing and (in honesty) we have a collective ability to be standing outside somewhere and still not be 100% sure if we've found it! So, in our own miniature Python sketch, we entered one of many Broadway Theatre stores. "Excuse me," I asked, "but where is the Shubert Theatre?" The girl looked straight at me and replied, "easy, it's just down Shubert Alley." A silly question, I guess? But with luck, Shubert Alley was in sight of the shop in question, so before too long we had tickets. By sheer good luck, we caught a performance that included the original Broadway cast (including Tim Curry, David Hyde Pierce, Hank Azaria and Sara Ramirez) and it was incredible, everything we'd wished it to be and more. Of course we had to go straight back to our hotel by taxi due to the large amount of Python memorabilia on sale (see my intro, if you haven't already sussed it out yet!) but hey, what a day.

We had intended to have the new CD catalogue in the shops by Christmas 2005, but with one Python shooting BBC documentaries (Terry Jones), another committed to James Bond or Harry Potter or possibly even both (John Cleese), a third at the helm of a PR campaign for the highest grossing musical to hit Broadway in years (Eric Idle) and a fourth having just signed a publishing deal to reproduce his diaries (Michael Palin), starting with the Python years, it was looking uncertain! In a typical Gilliam twist, Terry is busy promoting more than one movie in various parts of the world throughout the year, including *The Brothers Grimm*. Not even a little thing like death stands in the way of the Pythons, because Graham Chapman produced another best-selling book in 2005, *Calcium Made Interesting* (Sidgwick & Jackson), with (of course) a large dollop of help from Jim Yoakum, who is very much still alive. So we decided that perfection took time, and placed the whole thing on the temporary back burner. The intention now is to issue the eight original albums (with bonuses) by Easter of 2006, in the hope that the unissued album will be in shops in time for the Christmas holidays of the same year. I hope that by the time you read this, at least half of the CDs will already be in your collection. My fingers are crossed...

Finally, I'd like to say a big 'thank you' to Andre and all the team at Redwood for making me feel so welcome every time I turn up, even if sometimes it's for little more than coffee! And thanks for your encouragement on this project, mate, it means a lot.

Alan Parker
(We reached 'the end' without a Spanish Inquisition!)

APPENDICES:

APPENDIX ONE:
THE PYTHONS

MICHAEL PALIN The youngest Python by a matter of weeks, Palin is often labelled 'the nice one'. He attended Oxford, where he met his Python writing partner Terry Jones. The two also wrote the series *Ripping Yarns* together. Palin and Jones originally wrote together, but soon found it was more productive to write apart and then come together and review what the other had written. Therefore, Jones and Palin's sketches tended to be more focused than that of the other four, taking one bizarre, hilarious situation, sticking to it, and building on it. Examples include the 'Spanish Inquisition' sketch and the 'Mr Creosote' sketch in *The Meaning of Life*. These sketches take everyday situations (talking in the sitting room, dining out) but then introduce an unexpected, impossible to predict rogue element (the Spanish Inquisition, a grotesquely overweight man). From here, Palin and Jones could play around with the newly created environment, taking it to impossible, unbelievably stupid extremes, for example, attempting to torture old ladies with cushions or having Cleese's waiter feed Mr Creosote until he actually explodes, showering the other diners in viscera. In recent years, Palin has starred in a number of documentary travel series for the BBC in which he visits various – usually remote – locales, often along some predetermined route, as in his series *Pole to Pole* and the BBC sponsored *Around the World in Eighty Days*, where he followed the route of the fictional journey of Phileas Fogg in Jules Verne's novel of the same name. Palin is one of the most popular personalities in Britain today.

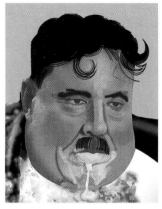

TERRY JONES All the Pythons have an eclectic range of talents, but Terry Jones is particularly hard to compartmentalise. George Perry has commented that should you "speak to him on subjects as diverse as fossil fuels, or Rupert Bear, or mercenaries in the Middle Ages or Modern China... in a moment you will find yourself hopelessly out of your depth, floored by his knowledge." However, not everyone considers Jones a show off, merely that he has a good-natured enthusiasm. It is this same good-natured enthusiasm that has led to his unflagging loyalty to the preservation of the group. As long as there is Terry Jones, there will be, in some way, a Monty Python. Jones' dedication to Python is not a recent occurrence, however. As well as writing with Michael Palin, he committed himself to directing the Python films *Monty Python and the Holy Grail* and *Life of Brian*, when it was felt that a member of the group should be in charge. Though the rest of the group appreciate such efforts, it would be a lie to say that there was not a little resentment at being bossed around by a man they viewed as an equal, especially when he acted as director. This has resulted in light-hearted joking at Jones' expense: Eric Idle, for example, constantly hails him as the most boring man on the planet. Of Jones' innumerable contributions to the show, his parodic, screechy-voiced depictions of middle-aged women are among the most memorable.

ERIC IDLE Two writing partnerships were absorbed into the Pythons – John Cleese and Graham Chapman, Terry Jones and Michael Palin. That left Terry Gilliam in his own corner, considered to be a sensible position in view of the arcane nature of his work, and Eric Idle. Idle was content to be cast as the group loner, preferring to write by himself, at his own pace, although he sometimes found it difficult in having to present material to the others and make it seem funny without the back-up support of a partner. Cleese claimed that, though he often felt his position was unfair, Idle was an independent person and worked best on his own. Idle claimed, "It was easier in a show where there were thirteen in a series than with a film, where stuff was read out all the time, and you had to convince five others. And they were not the most un-egotistical of writers either." Idle studied at Cambridge, a year behind John Cleese and Graham Chapman. His participation was essential to the Python synergy. His talent for verbal humour is exceptional, leading the group to dub him 'master of the one liner'. As a performer he can master with ease tongue-twisting word plays that verge on impossibility. He is also a talented songwriter and accomplished guitarist with a real ear for lyrics and styles. This talent lent heavily to the Python's work, composing, amongst others,

'Always Look on the Bright Side of Life', which has become the group's signature tune. Idle is currently the writer of the Broadway version of *Monty Python and the Holy Grail*, named *Spamalot*.

JOHN CLEESE Perhaps the best known of the Pythons, Cleese attended Cambridge (after being expelled from Clifton College, Bristol for painting footsteps from a statue to a bathroom), where he met his future Python writing partner Graham Chapman. His work with Chapman was, aside from Gilliam's animations, perhaps the most surreal of the Pythons' work and almost certainly the most intentionally satirical. Unlike Palin and Jones, Cleese and Chapman actually wrote together, in the same room. Cleese claims that their writing partnership involved him sitting with pen and paper, and Chapman sitting back, not speaking for lengths at a time, but that when he did speak, it was often brilliant. Without Chapman's input, the 'Parrot' sketch would have been about the duller subject of a car (it is much harder to imagine Cleese throwing about a car in the same way he threw about the parrot). Their work often involved ordinary people in ordinary situations, doing incredibly strange and surreal things. For example, Cleese and Chapman transformed the ordinary sight of 'a civil servant in black suit and bowler hat [making] his way to work' into a bizarre, unforgettable scene; the straight-faced Cleese used his physical potential to its full force as the crane-legged civil servant performing an athletic, grotesque, utterly unique walk to his office at the 'Ministry of Silly Walks'. This sketch was in fact written by Palin and Jones, but Cleese made it his own, showcasing his talent for physical comedy (also famously used in *Fawlty Towers*) and playing characters who could remain serious, even straight-faced, whilst doing something utterly ludicrous. His role as Sir Lancelot in *Monty Python and the Holy Grail* also showcases this, as he fights his way through a castle to save a damsel in distress, much like, say, Kevin Costner in films such as *Robin Hood*, although completely oblivious to the fact that he is actually savaging wedding guests. Another popular device used by the two was highly articulate arguments over completely arbitrary subjects, such as in the cheese shop, the 'Parrot' sketch or the argument clinic. All of these roles were opposite Michael Palin, who Cleese often claims is his favourite Python to work with.

GRAHAM CHAPMAN Chapman was perhaps best remembered for taking on the lead roles in *Holy Grail*, as King Arthur, and *Life of Brian*, as Brian Cohen. The movie roles were fairly straight, the comedy deriving from the stereotypical lead in bizarre situations, encountering eccentric characters, still being played as serious, and unflinching.

These roles, however, were unusual for the Graham Chapman the public had come to know on the *Flying Circus*, where he figured as the tall, craggy pipe smoker who gave the impression of calmness, disguising a manic unpredictability as real in his characters as it was in reality. For behind the pipe-smoking, rugby-playing exterior lay an alcoholic, with whom the rest of the Pythons often had trouble dealing. This was one of the reasons that Cleese left the television show after series three. Chapman particularly had trouble filming *Holy Grail* in Scotland, where he got a case of delirium tremens, often called DTs. During his worst alcoholism, he was reportedly consuming two quarts of gin every day. However, by the time his definitive role of Brian arose, he was sober and continued to produce some of his best work with the Pythons. Graham Chapman died of cancer on 4 October 1989. Thanks to the nature of the other Pythons, he is now lovingly referred to as 'the dead one'.

TERRY GILLIAM Terry Gilliam started off as an animator and strip cartoonist; one of his early photographic strips for Harvey Kurtzman's *Help!* magazine featured John Cleese. Moving to England, he animated features for *Do Not Adjust Your Set* and then joined *Monty Python's Flying Circus* when it was created. As an American, he was the only non-British member. He was the principal artist-animator of the surreal cartoons that frequently linked the show's sketches together, and defined the group's visual language in other mediums. Gilliam's Monty Python animations have a very distinctive style. He mixed his own art, characterised by soft gradients and odd bulbous shapes, with backgrounds and moving cut-outs from antique photographs, mostly from the Victorian era. The style has been mimicked repeatedly throughout the years: in the children's television cartoon *Angela Anaconda*, a series of television commercials for Guinness Beer, the 'Jibjab' cartoons featured on *The Tonight Show With Jay Leno* and the television history series *Terry Jones' Medieval Lives*. The title sequence for *Desperate Housewives* and the visits to the land of the living in the computer game *Grim Fandango* are also highly Gilliam-esque. Besides doing the animations for the *Flying Circus*, he also appeared in several sketches, usually playing parts that no one else wanted to play (generally because they required a lot of make-up or uncomfortable costumes, such as a recurring knight in armour who would end sketches by walking on and hitting one of the other characters over the head with a plucked chicken) and played side parts in the films. He co-directed *Holy Grail* and directed short segments of other Python films (for instance, 'Crimson Permanent Assurance', the short film that appears before *The Meaning of Life*). Gilliam has gone on to become a celebrated and imaginative film director with such notable titles as *Time Bandits, Brazil, The Adventures of Baron Munchausen, The Fisher King, Twelve Monkeys* and *Fear and Loathing in Las Vegas* to his credit. His latest work is *The Brothers Grimm*, released in August 2005.

APPENDIX TWO: THE DVDS

The Best of Monty Python's Flying Circus Volume One (BBC/BBCDVD1005)
A compilation of sketches from the first series (transmitted between 5 October 1969 and 11 January 1970), this disc runs 96 minutes.

At Last the 1948 Show (Boulevard Entertainment 506092900416)
Two discs. Includes interviews with Terry Jones and Tim Brooke-Taylor, plus US and UK TV advertisements. These discs run 157 minutes in total.

Do Not Adjust Your Set (Boulevard Entertainment 5060092900478)
Two discs. Includes interviews with Terry Jones and Tim Brooke-Taylor, plus US and UK TV advertisements. These discs run 259 minutes in total.

And Now for Something Completely Different (Columbia CDR 10064)
A full 1 hour 25 minute print of the movie, presented in mono, although it's Dolby sound. There are no bonus cuts on this DVD.

Monty Python's Flying Circus DVD 1 (A&E AAE-70042)
Contains television episodes 1, 2 and 3. Runs 102 minutes.

Monty Python's Flying Circus DVD 2 (A&E AAE-70043)
Contains television episodes 4, 5 and 6. Runs 102 minutes.

Monty Python's Flying Circus DVD 3 (A&E AAE-70045)
Contains television episodes 7, 8 and 9. Runs 102 minutes.

Monty Python's Flying Circus DVD 4 (A&E AAE-70046)
Contains television episodes 10, 11, 12 and 13. Runs 135 minutes.

Monty Python's Flying Circus DVD 5 (A&E AAE-70048)
Contains television episodes 14, 15 and 16. Runs 102 minutes.

Monty Python's Flying Circus DVD 6 (A&E AAE-70049)
Contains television episodes 17, 18 and 19. Runs 102 minutes.

Monty Python's Flying Circus DVD 7 (A&E AAE-70051)
Contains television episodes 20, 21 and 22. Runs 102 minutes.

Monty Python's Flying Circus DVD 8 (A&E AAE-70052)
Contains television episodes 23, 24, 25 and 26. Runs 135 minutes.

Monty Python's Flying Circus DVD 9 (A&E AAE-70083)
Contains television episodes 27, 28 and 29. Runs 102 minutes.

Monty Python's Flying Circus DVD 10 (A&E AAE-70084)
Contains television episodes 30, 31 and 32. Runs 102 minutes.

Monty Python's Flying Circus DVD 11 (A&E AAE-70086)
Contains television episodes 33, 34 and 35. Runs 102 minutes.

Monty Python's Flying Circus DVD 12 (A&E AAE-70087)
Contains television episodes 36, 37, 38 and 39. Runs 135 minutes.

Monty Python's Flying Circus DVD 13 (A&E AAE-70089)
Contains television episodes 40, 41 and 42. Runs 90 minutes.

Monty Python's Flying Circus DVD 14 (A&E AAE-70090)
Contains television episodes 43, 44 and 45. Runs 90 minutes.

The Complete Monty Python's Flying Circus (A&E AAE-72952)
Sixteen-DVD set, includes every *Flying Circus* episode, as well as *Live at the Hollywood Bowl, Live at Aspen, Parrot Sketch Not Included* and the first episode of *Fliegender Zirkus*. Also includes bios, a 'Pythonism glossary', a Gilliam animation gallery, troupe career highlights and supplementary material.

Monty Python and the Holy Grail (Columbia Tristar/05276)
Two disc 'Special Edition' featuring the movie and a whopping twenty-five special features, the movie itself runs 89 minutes.

Monty Python and the Holy Grail (Columbia Tristar CDR 14164B)
The deluxe box set 'Collector's Edition'. Along with two discs, you'll also find a book of the screenplay, a set of postcards, a unique 35mm movie still. The movie itself runs 86 minutes, but once again this set is loaded with extras.

Monty Python Live! (A&E AAE-70353)
Box set containing two discs. The first disc features *Live at the Hollywood Bowl* and the later re-union gig *Live at Aspen*, while the second disc includes *Parrot Sketch Not Included* (a twentieth anniversary documentary) and the first of the two German episodes. Disc one runs 153 minutes. Disc two runs 117 minutes, and both discs have extra bonuses.

Monty Python's The Meaning of Life (Universal 8207245)
Two disc 'Special Edition' featuring the movie and a whopping nineteen special features. The movie itself runs 103 minutes.

The Life of Python (A&E AAE-70132)
Box set containing two discs. The first features 'A Veritable Potpourri of Python' (basically the whole BBC 2 twenty-fifth anniversary night), while the second disc includes 'The Lost German Episode'. Disc one runs 125 minutes. Disc two runs 43 minutes, and both discs have extra bonuses.

The Best of Monty Python and Live at Aspen (BBC DVD1793)
Four-disc box set (limited edition). Special features include 'Sing-a-Long Lumberjack Song', 'Palindromes', 'Biographies', 'Radio Times – The Original Billing', 'Photo Gallery', 'It's the Monty Python Story', 'Pythonland', 'From Spam to Sperm' and bonus sketches (originally transmitted on BBC 2's *Python Night*). The running time of this DVD set is 5 hours and 38 minutes.

Monty Python's Life of Brian (Criterion Collection 61)
Original DVD issue of this incredible movie, which includes eight bonus features. The movie itself runs 94 minutes.

Monty Python's Life of Brian (Columbia Tristar CDR 35385B)
The deluxe box set 'Collector's Edition'. Along with the disc, you'll also find a book of the screenplay, a set of postcards and a unique 35mm movie still. The movie itself runs 90 minutes, but once again this set is loaded with extras.

Monty Python's Fliegender Zirkus (Rainbow Entertainment RDVD 9903)
The two German episodes on one DVD. The whole disc runs 86 minutes.

Eric Idle's Personal Best (A&E AAE-71954)
The best sketches from Eric Idle, including a behind-the-scenes featurette, quizzes and personal 'second-best' sketches.

Michael Palin's Personal Best (A&E AAE-73257)
The best from Michael Palin, with extras.

John Cleese's Personal Best (A&E AAE-71813)
The best from John Cleese, with extras.

Terry Gilliam's Personal Best (A&E AAE-74518)
The best from Terry Gilliam, with extras.

Graham Chapman's Personal Best (A&E AAE-74519)
The best from Graham Chapman, with extras.

Terry Jones' Personal Best (A&E AAE-74517)
The best from Terry Jones, with extras.

 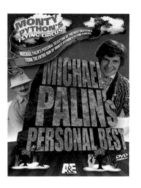 

APPENDIX THREE: THE CDS

Another Monty Python CD (Virgin Chattering VCCCD001, 1994 / Caroline 1107, 1997)
Trondheim Hammer Dance / Liberty Bell / Fanfare Opening / Formal Presentation / Contesana Padawana / Man of Power / Gold Lame / Southern Breeze / Spam Song / Bahama Parakeet / House of Fashion / Circus Tumble / Fanfare a / Mystery Drums / Mystery Place / Ode to Edward / In Step With Johann / Knees Up Mother Brown (To be re-released as EMI Records PYTHCD 1)

Monty Python's Previous Record (Virgin Chattering VCCCD002, 1994 / Caroline 1106, 1997)
Monty Python's Previous Record: Side One / Monty Python's Previous Record: Side Two (To be re-released as EMI Records PYTHCD 2)

Matching Tie & Handkerchief (Virgin Chattering VCCCD003, 1994 / Arista 18956, 1997) Salvation Fuzz / Elephantoplasty / Novel Writing Word Association / Bruces / The Adventures of Ralph... / Cheese Shop / Wasp Club / Tiger Talk / A Great Actor / Side 2: The Background to History / World War Noises in 4 / The Fight of the Century / Side 3: Minister for Overseas Development / Oscar Wilde and Friends / Taking in the Terrier / The Phone-In (To be re-released as EMI Records PYTHCD 3)

Monty Python and the Holy Grail (Virgin Chattering VCCCD004, 1994 / Arista 18958, 1997) Introduction to the Executive CD Edition / Tour of the Classic Silbury Hill Theatre / Live Broadcast From London: Premiere of the Film / Narration From the Silbury Hill Gentlemen's Room / You're Using Coconuts / Bring Out Your Dead / King Arthur and the Old Woman: A Lesson in Anarcho-Syndicated Commune Living / A Witch? / A Lesson in Logic / Camelot / The Quest for the Holy Grail / Live From the Parking Lot at the Silbury Hill Theatre / The Castle of Louis De Lombard: A Strange Person / Bomb Scare / Executive CD Edition Announcement / Another Executive CD Edition Announcement / The Story of the Film So Far / The Tale of Sir Robin / The Knights Who Say Ni! / Interview With Filmmaker Carl French / The Tale of Sir Lancelot: At Swamp Castle / Tim the Enchanter / A Shakespearean Critique / A Foul-Tempered Rabbit / The Bridge of Death / Executive CD Edition Addendum / The Castle Aaargh / The End (To be re-released as EMI Records PYTHCD 4)

Monty Python Live at Drury Lane (Virgin Chattering VCCCD007, 1994 / Caroline 1105, 1997) Introduction / Llamas (Including 'Granada') / Gumby Flower Arranging / Terry Jones-Link / Secret Service / Wrestling / Communist Quiz (Including World in Action) / Idiot Song / Albatross / Colonel / Nudge Nudge / Cocktail Bar / Travel Agent / Spot the Brain Cell / Bruces Song / Argument Song / Four Yorkshiremen / Election Special / Lumberjack Song / Theme Song 'Liberty Bell' / Parrot Sketch / Theme Song 'Liberty Bell' (To be re-released as EMI Records PYTHCD 5)

Monty Python's Life of Brian (Virgin Chattering VCCCD009, 1994 / Caroline 1104, 1997) Introduction / Brian Song / The Wise Men at the Manger / Brian Song (cont) / Sermon on the Mount (Big Nose) / Stone Salesman / Stoning / Ex-Leper / You Mean You Were Raped? (Nortius Maximus) / Revolutionaries in the Amphitheatre (Loretta) / Romans Go Home / What Have the Romans Ever Done for Us? / Ben / Brian Before Pilate (Throw Him to the Floor) / Prophets / Beard Salesman / Brian's Prophecy / The Hermit / He's Not the Messiah / He's a Very Naughty Boy / Pilate Sentences Brian / Nissus Wettus / Pilate Sentences Brian / Nissus Wettus With the Gaolers / Release Brian / Not So Bad Once You're Up / Revs Salute Brian / Cheeky is Released / Mandy to Her Son / Look on the Bright Side of Life (All Things Dull and Ugly) (To be re-released as EMI Records PYTHCD 6)

Monty Python's The Meaning of Life (Virgin Chattering VCCCD010, 1994 / EMI, 1994) The Meaning of Life / The Miracle of Birth / Every Sperm is Sacred / Growth and Learning / Fighting Each Other / Terry Gilliam Introduction (Accountancy Shanty) / Live Organ Transplants (Galaxy Song) / The Autumn Years (The Not Noel Coward Song) / Death / Dedication to Fish (To be re-released as EMI Records PYTHCD 7)

Contractual Obligation (Virgin Chattering VCCCD008, 1994 / Arista 18955, 1997) Sit On My Face / Announcement / Henry Kissinger / String / Never Be Rude to an Arab / I Like Chinese / Bishop / Medical Love Song / Farewell to John Denver / Finland / I'm So Worried / I Bet You They Won't Play This Song on the Radio / Martyrdom of St Victor / Here Comes Another One / Bookshop / Do What John / Rock Notes / Muddy Knees / Crocodile / Decomposing Composers (To be re-released as EMI Records PYTHCD 8)

Monty Python Sings (Virgin Records Mont D1, 1992; original release date 1991) Always Look on the Bright Side of Life / Sit on My Face / Lumberjack Song / Penis Song (Not the Noel Coward Song) / Oliver Cromwell / Money Song / Accountancy Shanty / Finland / Medical Love Song / I'm So Worried / Every Sperm Is Sacred / Never Be Rude to an Arab / I Like Chinese / Eric the Half a Bee / Brian Song / Bruce's Philosophers Song / Meaning of Life / Knights of the Round Table / All Things Dull and Ugly / Decomposing Composers / Henry Kissinger / I've Got Two Legs / Christmas in Heaven / Galaxy Song / Spam Song

The Monty Python Instant Record Collection (Virgin/Charisma Records CASCD 1134, 1989) Includes tracks taken from *Another Monty Python CD, Previous Record, Holy Grail, Live at Drury Lane, Matching Tie and Handkerchief* and one previously un-issued track. The Executive Intro / Pet Shop / Nudge Nudge / Premiere of Film / Live Broadcast From London / Bring Out Your Dead / How Do You Tell a Witch / Camelot / Argument Clinic / Crunchy Frog / The Cheese Shop / The Phone-In / Sit on My Face / Bishop on the Landing / Elephantoplasty / The Lumberjack Song / Bookshop / Blackmail / Farewell to John Denver / World Forum / String / Wide World of Novel Writing / Death of Mary Queen of Scots / Never Be Rude to an Arab

Monty Python's Spamalot (Decca Records 9880253, 2005) Original Broadway cast recording: Tuning / Overture / Historian's Introduction to Act I / Finland / Fisch Schlapping Dance / Monks Chant / He Is

Not Dead Yet / Come With Me / Laker Girls Cheer / The Song That Goes Like This / He Is Not Dead Yet – Play Off / All for One / Knights of the Round Table / The Song That Goes Like This (Reprise) / Find Your Grail / Run Away! / The Intermission / Historian's Introduction to Act II / Always Look on the Bright Side of Life / Brave Sir Robin / You Won't Succeed On Broadway / Diva's Lament (What Ever Happened to My Part?) / Where Are You? / His Name Is Lancelot / I'm All Alone / Twice in Every Show / Act II Finale / Always Look on the Bright Side of Life – Company Bow

Monty Python's The Final Rip-Off (Virgin 86033, 1992) Two disc set, perhaps the ultimate Python compilation. Disc One: Introduction / Constitutional Peasant / Fish Licence / Eric the Half-a-Bee Song / Finland Song / Travel Agent / Are You Embarrassed Easily? / Australian Table Wines / Argument / Henry Kissinger Song / Parrot (Oh, Not Again) / Untitled / Sit On My Face / Undertaker / Novel Writing (Live From Wessex) / Untitled / String / Bells / Traffic Lights / Cocktail Bar / Four Yorkshiremen / Election Special / Lumberjack Song / Untitled. Disc Two: I Like Chinese / Spanish Inquisition Part 1 / Cheese Shop / Cherry Orchard / Architect's Sketch / Spanish Inquisition Part 2 / Spam / Spanish Inquisition Part 3 / Comfy Chair / Famous Person Quiz / You Be the Actor / Nudge Nudge / Cannibalism / Spanish Inquisition Revisited / I Bet You They Won't Play This Song on the Radio / Bruces Song / Bookshop / Do Wot John / Rock Notes / I'm So Worried / Crocodile / French Taunter / Marilyn Monroe / Swamp Castle / French Taunter Part 2 / Last Word

Monty Python Live at City Center (Arista 18957, 1997) Introduction / The Llama / Gumby Flower Arranging / Short Blues / Wrestling / World Forum / Albatross / Colonel Stopping It / Nudge Nudge / Crunchy Frog / Bruces Song / Travel Agent / Camp Judges / Blackmail / Protest Song / Pet Shop / Four Yorkshiremen / Argument Clinic / Death of Mary Queen of Scots / Salvation Fuzz / Lumberjack Song

Monty Python's Flying Circus BBC Radio Collection (BBC Records ZBBC 2212CD, 1998) Flying Sheep / A Man With Three Buttocks / Crunchy Frog / Nudge Nudge Wink Wink / The Mouse Problem / Buying A Bed / Interesting People / Barber Shop Sketch / Lumberjack Song / Interview / Arthur Two Sheds / Children's Stories / Visitors / Albatross / Mr Hitler / The North Minehead By-Election / Me, Doctor / Dead Parrot Sketch / Self-Defence

The Pythons Autobiography by the Pythons (Orion 9 780752 860657, 2003) Two and a half hours of essential interviews. Taken from the tapes that made up the book of the same name.

Eric Idle Sings Monty Python (Restless 73730, 2000) Spam Song / The Meaning of Life / Money Song / Every Sperm Is Sacred / Accountancy Shanty / The Meaning of Life Poem / I Like Chinese / The Bruces' Philosophers Song / Men Men Men / Shopping / Sit on My Face / Penis Song / All Things Dull and Ugly / Eric the Half a Bee / One Foot in the Grave / I Must be in Love / Rock Notes / The Galaxy Song / Medical Love Song / Always Look on the Bright Side of Life / (Encore) Lumberjack Song / Liberty Bell And the new compilation of previously unreleased Python material: Hastily Cobbled Together for a Fast Buck! (To be released as EMI Records PYTHCD 9)

APPENDIX FOUR: THE BOOKS

And now for something completely analogue – the following books were published by Monty Python, mostly in large format:

Monty Python's Big Red Book Hardcover and paperback. Covers vary. London: Eyre Methuen, 1971. New York: Warner, 1975.

The Brand New Monty Python Bok London: Eyre Methuen, 1973. Chicago: Henry Regnery, 1976. (Paperback edition issued as *The Brand New Monty Python Papperbok*.) London: Eyre Methuen, 1974. New York: Warner, 1976.

Monty Python and the Holy Grail (Original and shooting script, with Gilliam pictures, lobby cards, stills, correspondence and cost breakdown.) London: Eyre Methuen, 1977.

The Life of Brian of Nazareth/Montypythonscrapbook (1979) (Film script plus a lot of extra material published back-to-back with it.) London: Eyre Methuen, 1979. New York: Grosset and Dunlap, 1978.

The Life of Brian script book published separately as a standard paperback New York: Ace, 1979.

Monty Python's The Meaning of Life (1983) (Film script with photos.) London: Mandarin, 1983. New York: Grove/Atlantic, 1983.

Monty Python: Just the Words (Full transcripts of all 4 television series. Originally published in two volumes.) London: Eyre Methuen, 1989.

The Complete Works of Shakespeare and Monty Python: Vol. 1 – Monty Python (A repackaging of both *The Big Red Book* and *The Brand New Bok*.) London: Book Club Associates, 1981.

The Fairly Incomplete & Rather Badly Illustrated Monty Python Songbook (By Terry Gilliam, Gary Marsh, John Hurst.) London: Mandarin, 1995. New York: Perennial, 1995.

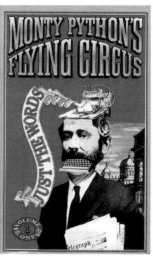

A Pocketful of Python, picked by Terry Jones (Terry Jone's favourite moments from the Python films and TV series.) Terry Jones, London: Methuen, 1999.

A Pocketful of Python, picked by John Cleese (John Cleese's favourite moments from the Python films and TV series.) John Cleese, London: Methuen, 1999.

A Pocketful of Python, picked by Terry Gilliam (Terry Gilliam's favourite Python moments.) Terry Gilliam, London: Methuen, 2000.

A Pocketful of Python, picked by Michael Palin (Michael Palin's favourite Python moments.) Michael Palin, London: Methuen, 2000.

A Pocketful of Python, hand-picked by Eric Idle (Eric Idle's favourite Python moments.) Eric Idle, London: Methuen, 2002.

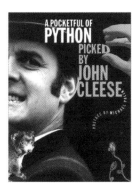 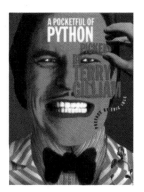  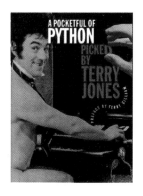

 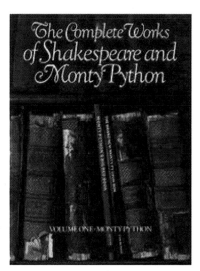 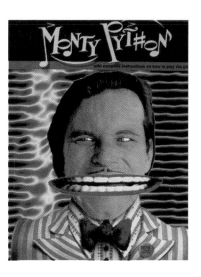

Further Reading:

From Fringe to Flying Circus, Roger Wilmut.
London: Eyre Methuen, 1980.

Monty Python: The Case Against Irreverence, Scurrility, Profanity, Vilification and Licentious Abuse, Robert Hewison. London: Eyre Methuen, 1981. New York: Grove, 1981.

Monty Python: Complete and Utter Theory of the Grotesque, John O. Thompson. London: British Film Institute, 1982.

Life of Python, George Perry London: Pavillion, 1983. New York: Little Brown & Co., 1983

The First 20 Years of Monty Python, Kim 'Howard' Johnson
And Now for Something Completely Trivial: The Monty Python Trivia and Quiz Book, Kim 'Howard' Johnson. New York: St Martin's Press, 1989. London: Plexus, 1990.

Monty Python: A Chronological Listing of the Troupe's Creative Output and Articles and Reviews About Them, 1969-89, Douglas L. McCall Jefferson: McFarland and Company, 1991.

Life Before and After Monty Python: The Solo Flights of the Flying Circus, Kim 'Howard' Johnson. New York: St Martin's Press, 1993. London: Plexus, 1993.

Monty Python's Complete Waste of Time: An Official Compendium of Answers to Ruddy Questions Not Normally Considered Relevant to Mounties!, Rusel Demaria. New York: Random House, 1995.

The First 28 Years of Monty Python, Kim 'Howard' Johnson. New York: St Martin's Press, 1999.

Monty Python Speaks!, David Morgan. New York: Harper, 1999. London: Ted Smart, 1999.

The (Non-Inflatable) Monty Python TV Companion, Jim Yoakum Nashville: Dowling, 1999. London: Right Recordings Limited, 2000.

The Pythons Autobiography by the Pythons London: Orion, 2003. New York: St Martin's Press, 2005.

APPENDIX FIVE:
THE COMPUTER GAMES

Monty Python's Flying Circus: The Computer Game (1991)
A platform/shoot-em-up game in which you play D. P. Gumby on a quest to find all four parts of his brain. Throw fish at flying feet, learn a lesson on 'the larch', or play a quick game of 'Breakout', among other things. Virgin Mastertronic

Monty Python's Complete Waste of Time (1994)
Based on different bits from the Python world, including a Desktop Pythonizer, a game to discover the secret to intergalactic success and an interactive Monty Python show. 7th Level

Monty Python and the Quest for the Holy Grail (1996)
A comedy-strategy adventure game based on the film *Monty Python and the Holy Grail.* 7th Level

Monty Python's 'The Meaning of Life' (1997)
A first-person puzzle solver in the style of *Myst* and loosely based on the Python film of the same name. SouthPeak Interactive

(– From *Wikipedia.com*)

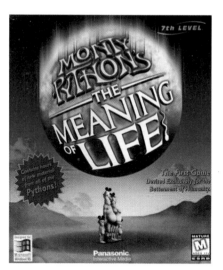

APPENDICES

APPENDIX SIX: HANDPICKED SOLO PERFECTION

Obviously, these choices are the author's only. Please feel free to check them out, and expand upon them with any choices of your own...

Eric Idle

The Rutles: All You Need Is Cash
Nuns on the Run
Wind in the Willows
Splitting Heirs
The Rutles 2: Can't Buy Me Lunch
The Adventures of Baron Munchausen

Michael Palin

Around the World in 80 Days (BBC TV)
Jabberwocky
The Missionary
A Fish Called Wanda
Ripping Yarns (BBC TV)
Fierce Creatures

Terry Jones

Personal Services
Ripping Yarns (BBC TV)
Wind in the Willows
Erik the Viking
Secret Policeman's Other Ball
Crusades

Terry Gilliam

Jabberwocky
Time Bandits
Twelve Monkeys
The Adventures of Baron Munchausen
Brothers Grimm
The Fisher King

Graham Chapman

The Odd Job
At Last the 1948 Show (BBC TV)
Yellowbeard
How to Irritate People
The Secret Policeman's Other Ball

John Cleese

Fawlty Towers (BBC TV)
A Fish Called Wanda
Fierce Creatures
Clockwise
Privates on Parade
The Magic Christian

APPENDIX SEVEN: ONLINE RESOURCES

For further information, updates or just plain shopping, check out:

www.pythononline.com
www.dailyllama.com
www.montypythonsspamalot.com
www.montypythonpages.com
www.intriguing.com/mp/
www.mwscomp.com/python.html
bau2.uibk.ac.at/sg/python/monty.html
www.serve.com/bonzai/monty/

ABOUT THE AUTHORS:

Alan Parker resides in the Maida Vale area of London, has written a number of books and works as a consultant with (among others) EMI Records, Secret Music and Universal Records. As a journalist he has contributed to *Record Collector, Mojo, Uncut, Spiral Scratch, The Zone, ICE, Bizarre* and a huge bunch of fanzines. His fascination with music and movies goes all the way back to the tender age of nine, and his mates are convinced he lives in a museum! A huge fan of Charles Dickens, he lists among his hobbies literally walking the streets of London to learn more. In more recent years he has become equally fascinated with the city of New York. He numbers a Monty Python dead parrot among his favourite items, and it's his only pet since the battery controlled goldfish died!

Mick O'Shea is forty-three years old. He lives with his wife Jakki in his hometown of Accrington, Lancashire, and still works a regular nine-to-five as a finance broker at Compass Finance Plc. *And Now for Something Completely Digital* is Mick's third published work to date, albeit as a co-author. His previous books are *The Zootopia Tree* (2002), which is a fantasy adventure featuring his two cats Sid and Oscar, and *Only Anarchists Are Pretty* (2004), which is a brand new take on the early career of the Sex Pistols. He has also produced articles for various magazines such as *Record Collector, The Zone* and *Amped*.

Like Alan, Mick has also enjoyed a long-standing love affair with music, and although his all-time favourite group has to be the Sex Pistols (he still rates the group's seminal *Never Mind the Bollocks* as the best album ever recorded), other groups, such as The Clash, Guns n' Roses and Stiff Little Fingers, are equally worthy of special mention.

Previous Books by Alan Parker:
Sid's Way: The Life & Death of Sid Vicious (Omnibus Press) with Anne Beverley
Satellite: Sex Pistols (Abstract Sounds) with Paul Burgess
The Great Train Robbery Files (Abstract Sounds) with Bruce and Nick Reynolds
Rat Patrol From Fort Bragg: The Clash (Abstract Sounds)
Song by Song: Stiff Little Fingers (Sanctuary) with Jake Burns
John Lennon and the FBI Files (Sanctuary) with Phil Strongman
Vicious: Too Fast To Live (Creation)
The Who by Numbers (Helter Skelter) with Steve Grantley
Flowers in the Dustbin: Sex Pistols (Helter Skelter)
Pretty Vacant: A History of Punk (Orion) with Phil Strongman
Punk Attitude (Carlton Books) with Don Letts
Come on Feel the Noize: Slade (Carlton Books) with Steve Grantley
Sid Vicious: Twenty-First Century Icon (Orion) with a foreword by Malcolm McLaren (Coming September 2007)

Previous Books by Mick O'Shea:
Only Anarchists Are Pretty (Helter Skelter)
The Zootopia Tree (Abstract Sounds Publishing)

WIKIPEDIA

Some sidebar and Appendix entries included in this text are derived from Wikipedia The Free Encyclopedia.

Wikipedia:Text of the GNU Free Documentation License Version 1.2, November 2002

Copyright (C) 2000,2001,2002 Free Software Foundation, Inc.

59 Temple Place, Suite 330, Boston, MA 02111-1307 USA
Everyone is permitted to copy and distribute verbatim copies of this license document, but changing it is not allowed.

PREAMBLE

The purpose of this License is to make a manual, textbook, or other functional and useful document "free" in the sense of freedom: to assure everyone the effective freedom to copy and redistribute it, with or without modifying it, either commercially or noncommercially. Secondarily, this License preserves for the author and publisher a way to get credit for their work, while not being considered responsible for modifications made by others.

This License is a kind of "copyleft", which means that derivative works of the document must themselves be free in the same sense. It complements the GNU General Public License, which is a copyleft license designed for free software.

We have designed this License in order to use it for manuals for free software, because free software needs free documentation: a free program should come with manuals providing the same freedoms that the software does. But this License is not limited to software manuals; it can be used for any textual work, regardless of subject matter or whether it is published as a printed book. We recommend this License principally for works whose purpose is instruction or reference.

APPLICABILITY AND DEFINITIONS

This License applies to any manual or other work, in any medium, that contains a notice placed by the copyright holder saying it can be distributed under the terms of this License. Such a notice grants a world-wide, royalty-free license, unlimited in duration, to use that work under the conditions stated herein. The "Document", below, refers to any such manual or work. Any member of the public is a licensee, and is addressed as "you". You accept the license if you copy, modify or distribute the work in a way requiring permission under copyright law.

A "Modified Version" of the Document means any work containing the Document or a portion of it, either copied verbatim, or with modifications and/or translated into another language.

A "Secondary Section" is a named appendix or a front-matter section of the Document that deals exclusively with the relationship of the publishers or authors of the Document to the Document's overall subject (or to related matters) and contains nothing that could fall directly within that overall subject. (Thus, if the Document is in part a textbook of mathematics, a Secondary Section may not explain any mathematics.) The relationship could be a matter of historical connection with the subject or with related matters, or of legal, commercial, philosophical, ethical or political position regarding them.

The "Invariant Sections" are certain Secondary Sections whose titles are designated, as being those of Invariant Sections, in the notice that says that the Document is released under this License. If a section does not fit the above definition of Secondary then it is not allowed to be designated as Invariant. The Document may contain zero Invariant Sections. If the Document does not identify any Invariant Sections then there are none.

The "Cover Texts" are certain short passages of text that are listed, as Front-Cover Texts or Back-Cover Texts, in the notice that says that the Document is released under this License. A Front-Cover Text may be at most 5 words, and a Back-Cover Text may be at most 25 words.

A "Transparent" copy of the Document means a machine-readable copy, represented in a format whose specification is available to the general public, that is suitable for revising the document straightforwardly with generic text editors or (for images composed of pixels) generic paint programs or (for drawings) some widely available drawing editor, and that is suitable for input to text formatters or for automatic translation to a variety of formats suitable for input to text formatters. A copy made in an otherwise Transparent file format whose markup, or absence of markup, has been arranged to thwart or discourage subsequent modification by readers is not Transparent. An image format is not Transparent if used for any substantial amount of text. A copy that is not "Transparent" is called "Opaque".

Examples of suitable formats for Transparent copies include plain ASCII without markup, Texinfo input format, LaTeX input format, SGML or XML using a publicly available DTD, and standard-conforming simple HTML, PostScript or PDF designed for human modification. Examples of transparent image formats include PNG, XCF and JPG. Opaque formats include proprietary formats that can be read and edited only by proprietary word processors, SGML or XML for which the DTD and/or processing tools are not generally available, and the machine-generated HTML, PostScript or PDF produced by some word processors for output purposes only.

The "Title Page" means, for a printed book, the title page itself, plus such following pages as are needed to hold, legibly, the material this License requires to appear in the title page. For works in formats which do not have any title page as such, "Title Page" means the text near the most prominent appearance of the work's title, preceding the beginning of the body of the text.

A section "Entitled XYZ" means a named subunit of the Document whose title either is precisely XYZ or contains XYZ in parentheses following text that translates XYZ in another language. (Here XYZ stands for a specific section name mentioned below, such as "Acknowledgements", "Dedications", "Endorsements", or "History".) To "Preserve the Title" of such a section when you modify the Document means that it remains a section "Entitled XYZ" according to this definition.

The Document may include Warranty Disclaimers next to the notice which states that this License applies to the Document. These Warranty Disclaimers are considered to be included by reference in this License, but only as regards disclaiming warranties: any other implication that these Warranty Disclaimers may have is void and has no effect on the meaning of this License.

VERBATIM COPYING

You may copy and distribute the Document in any medium, either commercially or noncommercially, provided that this License, the copyright notices, and the license notice saying this License applies to the Document are reproduced in all copies, and that you add no other conditions whatsoever to those of this License. You may not use technical measures to obstruct or control the reading or further copying of the copies you make or distribute. However, you may accept compensation in exchange for copies. If you distribute a large enough number of copies you must also follow the conditions in section 3.

You may also lend copies, under the same conditions stated above, and you may publicly display copies.

COPYING IN QUANTITY

If you publish printed copies (or copies in media that commonly have printed covers) of the Document, numbering more than 100, and the Document's license notice requires Cover Texts, you must enclose the copies in covers that carry, clearly and legibly, all these Cover Texts: Front-Cover Texts on the front cover, and Back-Cover Texts on the back cover. Both covers must also clearly and legibly identify you as the publisher of these copies. The front cover must present the full title with all words of the title equally prominent and visible. You may add other material on the covers in addition. Copying with changes limited to the covers, as long as they preserve the title of the Document and satisfy these conditions, can be treated as verbatim copying in other respects.

If the required texts for either cover are too voluminous to fit legibly, you should put the first ones listed (as many as fit reasonably) on the actual cover, and continue the rest onto adjacent pages.

If you publish or distribute Opaque copies of the Document numbering more than 100, you must either include a machine-readable Transparent copy along with each Opaque copy, or state in or with each Opaque copy a computer-network location from which the general network-using public has access to download using public-standard network protocols a complete Transparent copy of the Document, free of added material. If you use the latter option, you must take reasonably prudent steps, when you begin distribution of Opaque copies in quantity, to ensure that this Transparent copy will remain thus accessible at the stated location until at least one year after the last time you distribute an Opaque copy (directly or through your agents or retailers) of that edition to the public.

It is requested, but not required, that you contact the authors of the Document well before redistributing any large number of copies, to give them a chance to provide you with an updated version of the Document.

MODIFICATIONS

You may copy and distribute a Modified Version of the Document under the conditions of sections 2 and 3 above, provided that you release the Modified Version under precisely this License, with the Modified Version filling the role of the Document, thus licensing distribution and modification of the Modified Version to whoever possesses a copy of it. In addition, you must do these things in the Modified Version:

A. Use in the Title Page (and on the covers, if any) a title distinct from that of the Document, and from those of previous versions (which should, if there were any, be listed in the History section of the Document). You may use the same title as a previous version if the original publisher of that version gives permission.

B. List on the Title Page, as authors, one or more persons or entities responsible for authorship of the modifications in the Modified Version, together with at least five of the principal authors of the Document (all of its principal authors, if it has fewer than five), unless they release you from this requirement.

C. State on the Title page the name of the publisher of the Modified Version, as the publisher.

D. Preserve all the copyright notices of the Document.

E. Add an appropriate copyright notice for your modifications adjacent to the other copyright notices.

F. Include, immediately after the copyright notices, a license notice giving the public permission to use the Modified Version under the terms of this License, in the form shown in the Addendum below.

G. Preserve in that license notice the full lists of Invariant Sections and required Cover Texts given in the Document's license notice.

H. Include an unaltered copy of this License.

I. Preserve the section Entitled "History", Preserve its Title, and add to it an item stating at least the title, year, new authors, and publisher of the Modified Version as given on the Title Page. If there is no section Entitled "History" in the Document, create one stating the title, year, authors, and publisher of the Document as given on its Title Page, then add an item describing the Modified Version as stated in the previous sentence.

J. Preserve the network location, if any, given in the Document for public access to a Transparent copy of the Document, and likewise the network locations given in the Document for previous versions it was based on. These may be placed in the "History" section. You may omit a network location for a work that was published at least four years before the Document itself, or if the original publisher of the version it refers to gives permission.

K. For any section Entitled "Acknowledgements" or "Dedications", Preserve the Title of the section, and preserve in the section all the substance and tone of each of the contributor acknowledgements and/or dedications given therein.

L. Preserve all the Invariant Sections of the Document, unaltered in their text and in their titles. Section numbers or the equivalent are not considered part of the section titles.

M. Delete any section Entitled "Endorsements". Such a section may not be included in the Modified Version.

N. Do not retitle any existing section to be Entitled "Endorsements" or to conflict in title with any Invariant Section.

O. Preserve any Warranty Disclaimers.

If the Modified Version includes new front-matter sections or appendices that qualify as Secondary Sections and contain no material copied from the Document, you may at your option designate some or all of these sections as invariant. To do this, add their titles to the list of Invariant Sections in the Modified Version's license notice. These titles must be distinct from any other section titles.

You may add a section Entitled "Endorsements", provided it contains nothing but endorsements of your Modified Version by various parties--for example, statements of peer review or that the text has been approved by an organization as the authoritative definition of a standard.

You may add a passage of up to five words as a Front-Cover Text, and a passage of up to 25 words as a Back-Cover Text, to the end of the list of Cover Texts in the Modified Version. Only one passage of Front-Cover Text and one of Back-Cover Text may be added by (or through arrangements made by) any one entity. If the Document already includes a cover text for the same cover, previously added by you or by arrangement made by the same entity you are acting on behalf of, you may not add another; but you may replace the old one, on explicit permission from the previous publisher that added the old one.

The author(s) and publisher(s) of the Document do not by this License give permission to use their names for publicity for or to assert or imply endorsement of any Modified Version.

COMBINING DOCUMENTS

You may combine the Document with other documents released under this License, under the terms defined in section 4 above for modified versions, provided that you include in the combination all of the Invariant Sections of all of the original documents, unmodified, and list them all as Invariant Sections of your combined work in its license notice, and that you preserve all their Warranty Disclaimers.

The combined work need only contain one copy of this License, and multiple identical Invariant Sections may be replaced with a single copy. If there are multiple Invariant Sections with the same name but different contents, make the title of each such section unique by adding at the end of it, in parentheses, the name of the original author or publisher of that section if known, or else a unique number. Make the same adjustment to the section titles in the list of Invariant Sections in the license notice of the combined work.

In the combination, you must combine any sections Entitled "History" in the various original documents, forming one section Entitled "History"; likewise combine any sections Entitled "Acknowledgements", and any sections Entitled "Dedications". You must delete all sections Entitled "Endorsements."

COLLECTIONS OF DOCUMENTS

You may make a collection consisting of the Document and other documents released under this License, and replace the individual copies of this License in the various documents with a single copy that is included in the collection, provided that you follow the rules of this License for verbatim copying of each of the documents in all other respects.

You may extract a single document from such a collection, and distribute it individually under this License, provided you insert a copy of this License into the extracted document, and follow this License in all other respects regarding verbatim copying of that document.

AGGREGATION WITH INDEPENDENT WORKS

A compilation of the Document or its derivatives with other separate and independent documents or works, in or on a volume of a storage or distribution medium, is called an "aggregate" if the copyright resulting from the compilation is not used to limit the legal rights of the compilation's users beyond what the individual works permit. When the Document is included in an aggregate, this License does not apply to the other works in the aggregate which are not themselves derivative works of the Document.

If the Cover Text requirement of section 3 is applicable to these copies of the Document, then if the Document is less than one half of the entire aggregate, the Document's Cover Texts may be placed on covers that bracket the Document within the aggregate, or the electronic equivalent of covers if the Document is in electronic form. Otherwise they must appear on printed covers that bracket the whole aggregate.

TRANSLATION

Translation is considered a kind of modification, so you may distribute translations of the Document under the terms of section 4. Replacing Invariant Sections with translations requires special permission from their copyright holders, but you may include translations of some or all Invariant Sections in addition to the original versions of these Invariant Sections. You may include a translation of this License, and all the license notices in the Document, and any Warranty Disclaimers, provided that you also include the original English version of this License and the original versions of those notices and disclaimers. In case of a disagreement between the translation and the original version of this License or a notice or disclaimer, the original version will prevail.

If a section in the Document is Entitled "Acknowledgements", "Dedications", or "History", the requirement (section 4) to Preserve its Title (section 1) will typically require changing the actual title.

TERMINATION

You may not copy, modify, sublicense, or distribute the Document except as expressly provided for under this License. Any other attempt to copy, modify, sublicense or distribute the Document is void, and will automatically terminate your rights under this License. However, parties who have received copies, or rights, from you under this License will not have their licenses terminated so long as such parties remain in full compliance.

FUTURE REVISIONS OF THIS LICENSE

The Free Software Foundation may publish new, revised versions of the GNU Free Documentation License from time to time. Such new versions will be similar in spirit to the present version, but may differ in detail to address new problems or concerns. See http://www.gnu.org/copyleft. Each version of the License is given a distinguishing version number. If the Document specifies that a particular numbered version of this License "or any later version" applies to it, you have the option of following the terms and conditions either of that specified version or of any later version that has been published (not as a draft) by the Free Software Foundation. If the Document does not specify a version number of this License, you may choose any version ever published (not as a draft) by the Free Software Foundation.

INDEX